Advan

Becoming Strategic

"Developing a strategic approach to today's challenges has never been more important. This practical and welcome contribution really helps begin this vital process in daily business life."

—Bob Gorzynski, Author of *The Strategic Mind*,
Partner Wilde Geese Partnership, www.spiritofstrategy.org

"Action-provoking insights that can be immediately used! This is the kind of book busy leaders need to stay ahead of fast-paced change."

—Cláudia Schwartz, UCSD HR Leadership Program Director
Principle of HR Results, www.hrresults.com

"Many people talk about strategy. This book shows you how to live it! A MUST READ for anyone serious about turning strategy into profitable action."

—Michael Walsh, Business Strategist/CEO,
Thinking Big Is Not Enough
Kaizen Consulting Services Inc.,
www.kaizenconsulting.com

"Great job showing us how strategic thinking and planning can be energized and humanized with systems thinking at its core! A valuable read!"

—Sheridan L. Barker, Managing Partner
Haines Centre for Strategic Management
www.hainescentre.com

"More than a book this is a manual for leaders and followers, for those in transition and those who are lifers—this is a tour du force to assist the reader in truly impacting change by making a strategic difference."

—CB Bowman, MBA, CMC, MCEC
CEO: Association of Corporate Executive
Coaches http://www.acec-website.org

BECOMING STRATEGIC

LEADING WITH FOCUS AND INSPIRATION

TIMI GLEASON

This book was originally published in 2009 and titled Coach as Strategic Partner: A Survival Guide for Managers & Their HR Business Partners

Timi Gleason, Master Coach
24 Hours: 619-333-6945
StrategyCoach@ExecutiveGoals.com

Printed in the United States of America

Warning—Disclaimer
The purpose of this book is to educate and entertain. The author and/or publisher do not guarantee that anyone following these techniques, suggestions, tips, ideas, or strategies will become successful. The author and/or publisher shall have neither liability nor responsibility to anyone with respect to any loss or damage caused, or alleged to be caused, directly or indirectly by the information contained in this book.

Cover Art

This whimsical but take-charge weathervane reminds us of the message in this book:

- You can track the direction of a strategic conversation.
- You can learn how to introduce the strategic view point into any tactical conversation.
- You can become talented in your ability to contribute to strategy and vision.

Our weathervane is a photograph by Darlyne Murawski in Arlington, Massachusetts. Ms. Murawski has a doctoral degree in Biology from the University of Texas and a Masters of Fine Arts from the School of the Art Institute of Chicago. She is a highly published nature photographer and regular contributor to National Geographic Magazine. She has a passion for motivating a younger audience to explore the world of nature around them. To find out more about her acclaimed children's books and to view some of her other fascinating photography visit: www.darlynemurawski.com

Thank you to Ceanne Guerra for suggesting this wonderful metaphorical message!

I dedicate this book to
Krissy
who impressed everyone
with her strategic insights at age 18
during her first
strategic planning session
for Difference Makers International
and
to each of you who may never have the opportunity
to attend a formal strategic planning event,
but who have bosses and colleagues who
desperately need you to understand
what strategic thinking and planning are.
May you find courage and lightness
on your journey
and remember you are in good company.

Contents

Foreword

Many of us are living versions of the stories in this book. We are challenged to see work-related systems, a larger picture, and how everything is connected. Too often as leaders we become mired in the details of our work or the emotions of the challenges we are facing. We forget to take a step back, take a deep breath, and ask ourselves, "What was I trying to accomplish when I started this?" As strategists, what are we trying to accomplish? We get lost in the trees and can't see the forest. Every waking moment, we're confronted with the implications of a bigger picture in our lives, but so often we waste our opportunities to truly make an impact by fighting fires and missing the point.

Whether you are the CEO, a department head, an executive coach, or a human resources professional within an organization, your job is to focus on the long-term goals of the organization, the state of BEing for the company, while encouraging your team or clients to DO the necessary tasks that will help the organization achieve its desired state. Strategic thinking is about taking that step back to ponder the purpose—or end game—of any task, exercise, project, or meeting.

Through a series of examples and stories to elaborate the concepts, Timi Gleason illustrates the distinction between strategic thinking and analytical thinking–between the state of BEing and the act of DOing. Most of us are trained to be analytical and tactical. After all, it's tactics that win the game.....and we like to win... but without the whole team understanding the strategy behind the tactics, the end result isn't the anchored and stable outcome that would have moved us forward to new levels.

More and more CEOs are asking their leaders to be more strategic, but what IS that and how does one DO that?

In this book <u>Becoming Strategic</u>, Timi clearly lays the foundation to help coaches and managers understand the distinction between what is and isn't strategic behavior. Written in an easy style that makes you feel you're having a conversation, it's a book that is hard to put down and a reference you will turn to again and again.

Strategic thinking and systems thinking are two valuable 21st century skill sets. Partnering and collaborating skills are also critical to the future of our world. This book has both, and all of us who know Timi are glad to see her finally provide such a practical and user-friendly tool!

—Jeri Denniston
Chief Marketing Strategist with
Denner Group International,
www.dennergroup.com
jeri@dennergroup.com

Author's Note

THE HEART OF any company lies with its employees. Research shows that engaged employees and leaders are key to a healthy organization, and that in fact, a workforce that is not happily engaged often undermines financial success.

When employees are included in the design of the vision for their jobs and departments, the vision begins to unfold. Although our Boards, corporate headquarters or CEO may be profitability driven, and stubbornly focused on the bottom line, it is that "emotional mission" (the emotions behind the money) that drives engagement.

All too often there is no emotional connection or attempt to connect with the employees. Bosses may or may not communicate their financial goals and may not see a reason to ask their teams what it will take to BECOME the future. They just tell the employees what TO DO. There is nothing to feel personally proud of, or to celebrate. This book is about BECOMING the type of company that unifies employees around financial dreams.

Ideally, there is a Desired State that is attached to a journey of 18 months to 36 months of working towards that vision. The decisions that occur are an aligned, step-by-step action steps that support the closure of the gap between the Current State and the Desired State. Without a clearly defined Desired State, there are only "pathless" tactics.

In most markets, 90% of leaders are focused on problem solving, firefighting, and following an "input-output" productivity model. They run their companies as if it is a group of isolated departments. This model is money driven and based on meeting financial goals (an Operating Plan). Many leaders who say they do strategic planning at their company, after thinking about it, admit that what they do is create an Operating Plan. They execute on what I call Pasta Productivity: whatever sticks to the wall is their flavor of the day. Their many ideas become the center of power struggles and turf wars. They waste time in misalignment. Sales and Marketing conversations dominate meetings when there should be a clear path that includes each functional area and utilizes everyone in the overall approach.

Anything you do next should be a response to addressing the specific gaps between where you are now and where you can imagine being next. What do you intend to create for your customers (or your employees? Or your family?) Although action steps are very important to being productive, jumping into problem solving and productivity isn't what needs to come first. If you want to stand out in today's market, you have to become clear about what you are creating by your actions.

To become strategic, one must step back and take a moment to visualize the future as *if* the future has already arrived. Some people might say that it requires us to become more intentional. We have to slow down and think about what we want to create and what we are doing. When we stand in the middle of something that is completed in our minds and hearts, we can hear, smell, taste, touch, and already see our success. Once there, it is time to consider what is needed to bridge the gap between creating the future and where you are now. The gap between the two becomes your path.

You have to start with the end in mind as Stephen Covey would say. Without your Desired State, you will not be able to create the magnet that will draw you into the experience of Becoming Strategic.

Timi

Chapter 1:
The
Tactical
Mindset

*"Part of being strategic
is being able to look at problems
from a broader point of view."*

MY FIRST EXPOSURE to partnering with my CEO began during an "on-the-job training" odyssey that lasted from 1984 to 1992. Without any formal leadership background or previous newspaper publishing experience, I found myself the first pick as a senior team member in a subsidiary of a *Fortune* 200 daily newspaper. It all seemed simple enough on the surface.

All they needed me to do was clean up the reputation of their troubled HR department and win over the employees in the production department before a union was successfully voted in. My first day was two weeks before the election. People would ask me, "How do you like your new job?" but that was not the right question. "Do you think you will survive your new job?" seemed to fit much better, and "the newness" stayed that way for about 18 months.

Several days prior to the union vote and after many interviews with employees in the weeks leading up, a department meeting was held so my CEO and the pro-union employees could have a final conversation. Then "management" would be formally cut off by the NLRB rules (National Labor Relations Board) regarding 72-hour pre-election contact.

I was modestly (translate that: invisibly) standing in the back of the room observing and listening. My attitude at the time was that my boss had the responsibility for this. But then a very intimidating thing happened to me. As one of the senior employees was speaking about what it would take for them to trust the company in the future, he pointed over the heads of the crowd and focused on me. The crowd divided like the Red Sea for Moses, and there I stood…nailed and frozen in time. With burning eyes and a loud voice, he said, "We want HER support too!" I think I must have nodded "yes." I hope I smiled.

I can't even tell you what I did to respond. I only remember how shocked I was to be considered and called out as part of the SOLUTION! I'd only been there two weeks. But obviously, I was part of their solution…and probably my boss' solution. I was probably the complete opposite of the last person, but I'll admit one thing for sure, I was incredibly naive and unsophisticated at that time.

As it turned out, only two people voted for the union (16-2 in our favor). It is an understatement to say that the outcome of the election was a relief, but my relief didn't last long. What was unusual about my circumstances was that I had two OTHER big issues working in the background against me. They were issues that I'm sure my boss hadn't considered.

Trial by Fire

First of all, I had never been in an HR Department before; nor had I run a department as a supervisor or manager previously. It was a bit amazing that I had been the one selected for this coveted position after competing against more seasoned HR professionals. Now I was the top person, a senior team member with a span of authority in 11 different disciplines. I had safety, training, events, benefits, compensation, and workers' compensation, besides employee relations and legal compliance. Eventually, I would have two additional weekly and twice-a-week newspapers in very diverse geographical areas spanning two counties.

- This was well before any requirements to be a SPHR (Senior Professional in Human Resources). I'm sure I was hired for my ability to relate to the employees and straddle the fence as an advocate between employees and the leaders, but it would be years before that strong skill set would be explained and recognized as a strategic advantage.
- I had no newspaper industry experience, and learned quickly that as newspaper people we would be running a daily race against time. If a customer showed up at a newsstand and the paper wasn't sitting there ready to buy, you had lost the sale to your competition. If the news was hot that day, but you didn't have it out on the street for the customers, then you lost revenue and heard from your advertisers. I had to learn to move quickly and be ready to turn on a dime just like the rest of the team.

- I was starting out in the middle 1980's in California where no lawsuits were being won by employers. Chief Justice Rose Byrd was in office and she was so pro-employee it was making headlines! Labor relations attorneys were scrambling to stay on top of the current legal decisions. Culturally, this was a critical time in the professional development of many leaders. At our location, we were coming out of the cowboy days (meaning we acted like a startup) and were realizing that it was time for us to get organized, work on our professionalism, and act with more accountability to our employees and to each other. We were learning how to have a bigger picture of our business, and because we were a smaller daily newspaper, we had lots of leaders who shot from the hip and asked questions later (the cowboy part). Our newspapers were trying to drop their unions. I was there before (and during) the start of cracking down on drugs in the workplace, and to my disappointment, I was finding baggies and razor blades on the premises. It was also the start of realizing that workplace violence was an issue, even at our little location. We were having trouble with all of it!

- To make things more interesting, our subsidiary (because of its smaller size) was a laboratory for new technology and growth. None of this had been mentioned when I was interviewing or really taken into consideration when I was offered the job. Why? Because there wasn't any strategy; my coworkers were fire fighters. It was just "stuff that happened" and it was up to us to figure it out. We began a pilot project for desktop publishing in all departments; 11 new benefits were introduced in an attempt to standardize national offerings; we expanded our production facilities by 400%; we participated in a technological shift towards complete production automation from the news floor to the printing presses; we instituted a complicated new security system; we became entangled in a national debate and legal fight over the hourly status of reporters (did you ever think Clark

Kent-Superman was hourly?); and during the heated court room drama between Clarence Thomas and Anita Hill on TV, I was investigating accusations of sexual harassment in the newsroom.

- Our ink-covered press operators, who did not use microwave ovens at home, would be eventually asked to learn to run a three-story printing press, operating it passively from a "quiet room" by evaluating and pushing computerized screens and buttons. They were terrified of being unable to learn the new technology.

The second issue was that our corporate offices in the Midwest had just become publicly held about six months earlier. It had shareholders to consider and a profit to report publicly. Part of the problem behind the union movement was that our long term employees could not get any accurate pension data. The corporation wasn't in compliance with ERISA law. Although my hands were tied on my end, I was to become the new voice of advocacy on behalf of the employees while our corporate offices scrambled to straighten things out. We were at tremendous risk of a lawsuit and being sued by ERISA, too…and keep in mind that emotions were already pent up, and distrust was rampant, well before I had arrived. They hated the last HR person.

However, I did have some things working in my favor. I was new, and to some extent the employees cut me some slack because I was responsive and honest about my end of the problems. But my "ramp up time" was steep and clearly perilous for my first two years. Did I need to learn how to become a strategic partner? You bet! The employees needed me, and so did my boss.

Following the positive outcome of the union movement there was an instant 400 percent increase in workers' compensation activity. It didn't seem to be intentional. In other words, there wasn't any doubt that the employees were legitimately injuring themselves… but why and how? I noticed that the injuries were largely in the areas of knees, feet, legs…all those parts of your body that move you forward. Part of being strategic is being able to look at problems from a larger point of view. The point of view I used was metaphysical. Louise Hay's book: <u>Heal Your Body</u>, discusses the mental causes of physical illness. It was a stretch and it was a shot in the dark, but from that piece of information I surmised that I had a group of people who were "concerned about their futures". How would they move forward professionally after this upset of the union movement and getting a new human resources director? There was some fear of retaliation, some job insecurity and for several of them, there was concern about whether their pension benefits would be there when they retired. It was clear that we needed to stick together and talk about the future more frequently and openly.

For what would become the next eight years of my career, we worked collaboratively to get through many difficult changes in culture and daily routine. At times it was very stressful and our solutions lacked any strategic vision. My learning curve was on a fast and furious track. Dependability, trust, authenticity, and frequent communication had to become our shared goal. Ultimately we got there and were stronger for it. But, at the corporate offices, it was not so smooth.

The Confusion at Corporate

Simultaneously, our corporate office was starting to get its act together. They knew they were out of compliance on ERISA and in other areas of national administration. They were realizing that they had shareholders who expected something that had never been provided when the company was privately held. The concept of "strategy" was first laid out by the corporate offices in the form of newly required metrics and measurements. These eventually evolved into requiring us to develop our analytical skills. We started to get "how to" presentations, but there was still no explanation of the desired state. Why were we doing all this work? What did they need from us? I am naturally strategic, so I wanted to know what the big picture was and no one could articulate it for me.

It was painful and confusing and unsettling to discover what "becoming strategic" meant. The application of strategy was new to everyone, and how to "explain it" and what it would "get us" in the end was not forthcoming. Tactically, it was understood that we needed more tracking, so we could predict where we were headed. From an empathy standpoint, no one had considered the importance of explaining these decisions to anyone who was going to have to execute the work. To be honest, the exercise of collecting the metrics seemed like busy work.

Looking back, we were "following a set of strategic steps from a tactical mindset." It would take me years to understand why everything that happened during that time was so difficult.

Making Distinctions

The new HR leader at corporate knew what to do to run the company better and to put us into compliance. What he didn't know was how to engage the hearts and minds of his leaders at the various properties by explaining the end game to us. If we had known what the vision was and how it was supposed to look and feel when we got there, we could have moved faster, helped him out, and perhaps, have felt more excited about all this new work!

We were part of 24 diversified newspaper, radio, television, newsprint and media properties throughout the United States and Canada. The corporate offices were trying to bring us into compliance as quickly as possible by telling us what to do. We were treated like "bad hires" because we were passive. We were passive because we didn't have enough information about where all this work was headed.

This is a big mistake that we make as leaders and strategic partners when we don't share the end game with our employees and colleagues. In our own inability to articulate our vision and needs, we expect smart people to be able to read our minds, and most of the time they can't. It is in this exact moment that we have the opportunity to help each other. If you are at the receiving end of this lack of communication, what can you do to help others express their ideas? How can you paraphrase what they may be thinking? How can you validate your shared, but unspoken alignment?

The Boss' Role

If you are the one who is frustrated with the blank stares you are getting, how can you draw out the questions? What can you do to talk out your thoughts with a trusted colleague before you go in front of your staff and lay out your wishes? Are you willing to articulate the end results that you want?

Several years into my tenure, we attended a summit meeting at our home offices in Chicago. All 24 property HR Directors were there. There were lots of "hints and threats" thrown at us in the course of the three day meeting. The big one was: "You all need to become more strategic!"

What did THAT mean? Although desktop computers were not the norm yet (this was the late 1980's), we learned that the chairman of the Board didn't use one, but the CEO had one and used it all the time. Were we as HR leaders supposed to learn them now? Desktop computers were something that our secretaries had. They needed them for spread sheet work. They printed out our reports for us. We were busy in meetings. How would these changes add up to the HR leaders becoming more strategic?

There were mixed messages everywhere. We were being nagged to "become more strategic or get out." But there were no specific behavioral changes suggested to us; no training was offered. Our ability to conform was assumed and expected. Not wanting to miss the opportunity to get on the bus, I followed up with the top person in our HR division and asked her if she could give me three-to-five specific behaviors that would help me understand what I could do differently. Painfully, she admitted that she couldn't. She was in the dark, too. That was puzzling and frightening to me! Why was this so mysterious? If I didn't break the code, then what would happen next? I found out quickly.

Within 90 days, our HR leader was replaced and our four-person Corporate HR Department grew to a massive department of 45 highly-driven individuals. We had employee relations attorneys, a union-busting team, benefits specialists, national risk loss managers, compensation gurus, all sorts of trainers and way too many new people demanding data from us.

The Good News

Over a few short years, I learned that being strategic involves:

- Tracking employee demographics and other important metrics or demographics
- Seeking out opportunities for "economies of scale"
- Setting up "centers of excellence" and promoting "standardization"
- Assuring national compliance with laws and regulations
- Keeping others from financially suing our "deep pockets"
- Tracking EEO so we aligned with community racial/ethnic populations
- Communicating data "up" so that further strategic thinking could occur

In retrospect it was a fabulously valuable education. I emerged eight years later a highly seasoned HR leader ready for a position in corporate human resources in a four diamond hospitality business…but it had definitely been a very harsh journey.

My story is the inspiration for this book. I know there are still companies and people out there who feel as clueless as I was then. You may even feel like a fake or a fraud. You may be in a very senior position and feel frightened of being "discovered" because you are confused about strategic thinking. I want to dispel your fear. The situation you are in is NOT hopeless and neither are you. It's time to stop worrying and keep reading.

* * *

NEXT: What is and is not considered strategic behavior?

Chapter 2:
Gutsy Conversations and Loaded Topics

*"To accomplish great things,
we must not only act, but also dream:
not only plan, but also believe!"*

—Anatole France

MOST PEOPLE DON'T distinguish between strategies and actions, even though the two words lead to different results. The vision of the future is our strategy. The steps we will take to get there are our actions, or tactical decisions.

Strategies are about BEING and tactical issues are about DOING. Strategy has become one of those words that we say and don't fully appreciate. We throw the word around without realizing that we are focused on problem solving and action, when sometimes we just need a clear idea of where we are creating.

While reading Chapter 1, you may have wondered how many years have passed since I was first confronted with trying to understand the concept of strategy versus tactics. When I realized that almost 30 years later, strategic thinking was still very confusing, I wanted to share what I have learned and accomplished. By design, most of us are problems solvers and tactically motivated. We work in industries where expertise is valued. We hire smart people who have great ideas. With the introduction of metrics, efficiencies, and visioning, we have discovered that the advantages of having a clear of idea of our future increases our profitability.

In today's world there are many gurus, books, and classes that can provide you with the technical guidance you may need to navigate through all the tactical steps of strategic planning and thinking. You can find out how to DO it, but still there is not much that brings explains why we need to develop a clear outcome before we get started. The gap between "what is" and "what could be" is the path. And although by position or title, your role may sound strategic, you may still not intellectually understand how to intentionally create strategic results.

If you feel pressured to be "more strategic," do you ever find yourself wondering out loud "What the heck do they want from me?!"

What Your Boss Wants

I believe that behaving strategically is still a problem for most people and that the confusion starts from the top. Most top bosses (and corporate groups) are struggling with their natural tendencies to be tactical and work in silos. The strategic thinkers are few and far between. So you have to go into this willing to struggle with it. And you need to know that you are definitely not alone. An important aspect of expressing strategy is that collaboration and sensory skills are needed.

Learning to think and behave as a strategic partner is a very valuable skill set in the 21st century because so much is changing around us. With all the unique problems we are facing with our economic situation, the climate, the labor market, and our futures in general, the more visionary and strategic you can be the better. Our world needs people who can balance out all the firefighting and problem solving that goes on 99% of the time.

Obviously action oriented problem solving has its value and advantages. Not much gets done without action and you can't reach a desired state without action steps. But all the action steps in the world won't get you anywhere without a desired state. Once you learn to be strategic, you will play a valuable role; or another way to say that is, you will become a valuable partner. Not that your road will be glamorous or celebrated; highly tactical people really struggle with letting go of their learned style. It takes extra work to learn to toggle between tactical and strategic adeptly. Don't be discouraged with yourself if you still feel a little out of your element, or others won't listen to you at first. Be a good listener and practice daily.

Remember These

We have laid out two important aspects of being strategic.

- You need to be genuinely interested in collaborating with others
- You need to learn how to develop a Desired State before you jump into problem solving your Current State (tactics)

Working on the Wrong Problems

As you learn to demonstrate and exercise your strategic skill level, you may become one of the few on your team who stimulates rich discussion and a broader point of view. You will also see a gradual need for your opinions and presence in key meetings. Your perspective will become valuable as you help others focus on the real issues and stay on the path. The PATH is the gap between the Desired State and the Current State.

Most leaders are still lingering in an area of vagueness about the psychological and emotional aspects of thinking and "being" a partner in their work life. Tactically, we approach "partnerships" with dutiful response, but emotionally and psychologically we don't really see the value of complicating our lives with "one more vote". But this isn't about votes. It's about discussing opportunities. Many of us still aren't willing to take the necessary risks to speak up when we see things differently. In order to make productive use of building a Desired State, imagining an end game has to come before working through any gaps or discussing Current State. Without a clear path (the gap between Current State and Desired State):

- we see problems one dimensionally and are often involved in working on the wrong problems.
- we can be pressured into acting without a clear outcome or alignment with others.
- we will hesitate to question our team mate's (including our boss') perception of a situation, or if we would consider it, we find we are not articulate enough in expressing a different point of view.
- we may be perceived as attacking another's ideas or competing against them, instead of brainstorming together about a clear path.

In essence, many people are frequently working on the wrong problems, and are focused on tactics instead of outcomes. There is a lot of mental spinning without a target. They want to know what will "put the fire out" not "what will help prevent fires". They don't ask if the fire is actually an immediate threat.

Strategy is about being inside of a future state. We learn to project the future into our current thoughts and potential actions. When we jump to conclusions without considering the larger consequences or our long range vision, we short-circuit our success.

What's a Desired State?

Strategic thinking considers a broader point of view, connectivity to shareholders and other functional groups, and includes having a bold end game in mind. Simple example: "We want to be in a committed relationship for the rest of our lives" vs. "we need to send out announcements, get married, buy a house, and get a dog." The Desired State is the dream and the feelings. It's not the arrival of the invitations or buying the dog we want.

Desired States aren't long documents, perhaps one half to three quarters of a page. They don't have much detail as a rule. They may be sensory and emotionally descriptive. The following are simple examples:

1. **Strategy: Become a slender and healthy person.** The action steps are specific decisions, milestones, and metrics related to diet, exercise, and health management.
2. **Strategy: Capture the imagination and hearts of children of all ages.** The action steps: build a place called Disneyland; start with a section called Tomorrowland, then add Adventureland, then Fantasyland with design details on the particulars of each.
3. **Strategy: First Choice of Customers with 60% of our market share in our industry.**
   The action steps: Hire and train a sales force, beef up telemarketing, provide warm leaders, increase social media, track

milestones and metrics, develop customer appreciation programs, and community outreach opportunities.

Creating a Desired State:
You Can't Have It if You Can't Imagine It

Being both strategic and a good business partner requires some extra time, but like planning any project that requires preparation, in the end you'll find you save time and pave your way to success when you handle the upfront planning.

Think about planning a wedding for 100 guests or a river boat trip to Europe. We automatically create a Desired State for these types of events. We engage emotionally in the excitement of the outcome, and our five senses imagine the fun, the special moments and the necessary steps we need to take to close the gap between today and then. Part of this sensory data is created by the promotional photos, positive quotes from satisfied customers, and some of it from pure imagination. An organization's Desired State requires the same attention to detail:

- Do you work in a call center? Imagine a quiet, calm call center; a team of I.T. people and call center leaders who have learned and can even anticipate why certain problems occur when lines go down. They become experts in bringing downed lines back up quickly. Stressful moments are handled with confidence and mastery. Customer service is affected minimally.
- Do you work in an operations department? Imagine a competent, well-trained team that masterfully tracks their projects, uses technology to solve problems, tracks results on an ERP system, and where each supervisor and employee is positioned for career advancement as part of the new generation of leaders. What are the steps they will follow to get there?

- Imagine a marketing department: They are dreaming of becoming highly regarded as partners for the call center, for sales, and for the customers, including government agencies and community leaders. They can imagine winning JD Powers awards for customer satisfaction and industry innovation. They can imagine driving their company to Number One in their market. To build stronger relationships with the company's customers, they imagine creating recognition programs for targeted groups of customers. From there, the action steps are put into place to create programs that bring recognition to customers for their hard work in the community. Criteria is established for deciding whether they will honor teachers, civil service workers, create fun events that include children, or possibly veterans. These types of decisions are tactical after the larger vision is established.

You Are Already There

Desired States are the epitome of practicing magnetic attraction. We step into the vision and imagine we are already there. Once a vice president confronted me about this; everyone in the room was all ears to hear my response. I had asked him to talk about the Desired State "as if it had already happened" instead of thinking about it in the future tense. I couldn't believe what I said when he said, "Why do I have to do that?!" Out came some unconscious brilliance: "Because you can't have it, if you can't imagine it!"

To do this, you need to speak as if you are three to six months past realizing your entire Desired State. Let me repeat that a bit differently: You have achieved your goal, and now you are basking for another three to six months since you got it. You can imagine the new ventures you can tackle next. You are done!

Trust me…if you can imagine the feeling of being done; if you are already there as you work your plan, the hardest part is the act of walking through the steps. When a Desired State is THAT clear within your group and within yourself, it is just a matter of time, and alignment is not an issue. Speaking up to your boss is not an issue, worrying about being "heard" is not a problem…because you are already THERE. The secret is to force your imagination to look forward and to experience your feelings of success ahead of time. **There are several powerful dynamics that are set into place by doing this:**

- **Subconscious Motion:** Whenever, we can visualize the finished product (or outcome) ahead of time, we are half way there already. The ability to feel and experience the success before we reach it sets the project in subconscious motion in a way that tactical planning <u>can't touch, can't duplicate, and can't compete with!</u>
- **Emotional Alignment:** Imagine the power of a whole group's mental and emotional alignment around a dream! *Every day* becomes a great day to wake up and go to work.
- **Structural Tension:** A tension between the Desired State and Current State has been created that will pull time and people invisibly towards the goal. "Hit and miss" is not a concern when there is a clear Desired State. Everything that happens is getting you there even if it is a crooked path, because you are clear emotionally and mentally.

Compare this top notch experience to experimenting with solutions as problems come up, and there's no end game in mind except "make it stop".

With a clear vision, the whole team knows the metrics and the best way to measure progress. It's easy to stay the course when your team is focused and clear about the end results.

Case Study: We Didn't See It Coming

A field operations department that I worked with put a 24-month plan into action with very clear metrics and milestones. They HAD to transform their operations and the level of talent they had, or else face serious consequences. I helped them write out how they would feel, and what it would mean to them to be successful. Looking back, what they planned to do was beyond belief in many ways. They had so far to go and so many changes to make.

Six months into it, we checked our plans. We were on target with very few delays, but the 18-month mark seemed impossible. At a year, we looked at the Desired State again and our action steps. We were making progress, but what we had written still seemed very distant.

At 18 months, so many disruptive things were pulling on us, that it was another six months before we stopped to discuss our progress. We didn't check at 18 months. When we finally sat down, we found ourselves at 24 months. The Director and I read the Desired State out loud as a way to see how we were doing, so we could discuss it and track what we had not completed.

We were dumbfounded. The Desired State sounded silly now. Somewhere in the last six crazy months, we had flown by our previous vision and were WAAAAY past our targets and into a completely transformed department.

We sat there in shock looking at a new world. When had we zoomed past GO, collected our $200 and entered a new reality? We had transformed and then some! Had we not revisited our written Desired State, we might not have realized how much we had changed, transformed, and evolved.

The Op's Director looked at me: "Timi, I have goosebumps. Wow, that's amazing!"

We really didn't have words for what had happened. Do you want to work in a dynamic work place and build those amazing moments with others? If so, let's start practicing!

Is the Approach Strategic or Tactical?

A committee was meeting to hammer out how they would change their reporting and tracking documents. They wanted to find a way to standardize their language and measurements:

- at the corporate level
- in the finance department, and
- at the department level.

Their efforts were ultimately going to be part of a larger effort to standardize much of the reporting vocabulary used with all departments. Currently monthly calls resulted in an apples and oranges conversation with no common ground or translation. This was a strategic issue.

They took a strategic opportunity and treated it like a problem to be solved:

- They don't have a long term strategy (Desired State) for standardizing these types of processes;
- They do have their best and busiest people working on it department by department;
- They have a group facilitator to manage their brainstorming process;
- They argue, they debate and brainstorm, and at times, they spin in circles.

How long do you think this will take them? Do you think they will ultimately standardize everything? Will they be energized by the process or dragged down and become tired of it? Can they replicate this process with other such standardization projects? (The answers are: A long time; too long. No. Burned out. Not a likely to spark any replication.)

What Happened

The task became a battle between subject matter experts instead of a partnership between great minds. Without a larger picture of all pieces of the standardization movement, and a sense of how the project impacts others outside of their own area, these important strategic questions never became a framework for success:

1. What types of opportunities will we create with a consolidated, standardized approach?
2. How might our jobs and budget change because of this new approach?
3. Who else will be affected by the consolidation effort, standardization, and attempts to change?
4. What other competing initiatives are coming that affect our decisions?
5. Will the various finished products ultimately enhance our teamwork?
6. Are there reports that are redundant or that we can eliminate?
7. Who else might be affected? Do we already have them involved in this?
8. Who are the cross-functional talents who need to provide input on consequences?

To behave strategically would imply that the team leaders are willing to proactively reach out to all stakeholders and cross-functional partners and seek buy-in on a broader basis. Although we can say that the group is technically working on a strategic issue (alignment through standardization), their approach is not strategic, but tactical and siloed.

Project groups set up as tactical groups tend to take much longer to get the job done. In my experience these groups:

- Become psychologically and physically de-energized as they struggle internally
- Struggle over right or wrong and good or bad outcomes and no not share a vision
- Show little to no effort to make standardization a companywide alignment issue that is being tackled in a uniform, collaborative manner

- Unintentionally, turn uninvolved stakeholders into future road blocks
- Lose members to higher priorities because they "don't have time for it". That should be your first clue that if the project has become an "it"; there's no Desired State firmly in place giving the team members inspiration to stay and see it through.

This is opposite of a group that starts out aligned and energized for success. If you start to see these things happen, stop and consider the real problem: no shared vision, siloed efforts, and a lack of communication.

As strategic thinkers, we need to be very clear about what we are intending to create: visually, emotionally, physically, and socially. Time is money. We need to do our upfront homework. With a Desired State, you can take a project from being a huge, complex issue to being accomplished in half the time. The group is energized around common goals. Energized groups thrive on accomplishment.

The Strategic Advantage

I think our hearts and souls become very numbed when we over-focus on reports, numbers, and data without executing them from a strategy. Although discussion of strategy requires an investment of time and one-to-one conversation, once in place, we make up for lost time with alignment and collaboration.

When we hesitate to question or argue for what we think is right, we lose: either we lose in terms of quality, or in terms of missing the opportunity to learn more about the problem. Your philosophical opinion is never as important as the discovery process.

We stand in awe of leaders and consultants who speak authoritatively in company jargon using words like "dash boards", "end-to-end processes", "legendary customer service" and "organizational change". They throw around words like "vision" and "strategy" (add in YOUR own company's favorites) but what remains missing is the upfront time and specific discussion about what the future success will look like when it is finished and done.

We miss the opportunity to build engagement and passion for our work. What do we think success will be like? Can we agree on that vision and does it excite us? The goal here is to become a person who is willing to take an extra moment to think beyond immediate problem solving and venture into discussing the consequences of our hard work.

What should we talk about in order to partner and collaborate strategically?

- Perceptions
- Repercussions
- Desired outcomes
- Sensory reactions
- Group values

By taking the time to fully connect to our passion for projects and by discussing the difference a successful outcome will make to, not only our bottom line but our lives, our communities and businesses, we can experience gratifying success and daily job satisfaction.

Avoiding Complications

What kinds of road blocks and push backs do we create when we ignore collaboration with others who may be impacted directly or indirectly by our decisions and actions? Do we consider other stakeholders in our field of influence? Our stakeholders are:

- Other departments
- Our vendors
- Our customers
- Our corporate office or Board of Directors
- Our family members at home, especially our spouse
- Sometimes, our neighbors

It's good if you are meeting your numbers. It's very gut-wrench-ing and disengaging if you are not. Do other non-collaborative team mates cause you to miss your goals, or is that what you do to them?

The next chapters are potential starting points for creating a bigger conversation with strategic results. From my point of view these are classic, foundational issues that operate and undermine every company at some time.

They are common issues that are not usually considered as get-ting in the way of strategy, but they do. They are loaded topics…the kind you'd rather not discuss, especially with your boss.

*   *   *

Our next considerations will examine how the economy and politics complicate our ability to behave strategically.

Chapter 3:
Eating Strategy for Breakfast— The Labor Market and the Economy

"It feels like we are riding a roller coaster though a long, dark tunnel. One hopes for some happy music at the end!"

The Economy

IN 2002 WHEN I was designing the course that later became the first edition of this book, our country was still staggering from a collapse of the dot com boom. And although we held high hopes for recovery of the market around October 2001, we then experienced 9-11 and the devastation of terrorism. Our grieving period was long. We then went to war.

Then by 2004, the real estate market started to boom and that diverted some people for a while. Strategists tried to warn us that it would be short-lived, but we had dollar signs in our eyes.

By 2008, a collapse was in full force, and ultimately we came to realize that our country had been betrayed by dishonest policy makers. Decisions that had been made in greed financially affected everyone, including our global neighbors. Seven years later, we are still struggling to renegotiate our lives. Our political climate is unrecognizable and frequently contentious. Although our standard of living still remains higher than in most countries, a large sector of Americans feel emotionally and financially robbed.

When you think of all the events that have impacted our plans and dreams in the last 10 years: war, the demise of corporate ethics, and now billion dollar and trillion dollar government bail outs…it feels like we are riding a roller coaster though a long, dark tunnel. One prays for some happy music at the end.

Is there an end? What is our country becoming? Or are we (again) just DOING the best we can as a nation. There doesn't appear to be political alignment or a long range dream for all Americans.

There were chances to stop and look at the big picture, consider outcomes based on our behaviors, and to put a long-range plan into action. But we were in a rush to stop this, start that, and hurry up. This is true for a vast majority of businesses in the United States.

The Labor Market

There were several developments unfolding simultaneously. Some were obvious and some are still relatively invisible to the average citizen. The year 2010 represented the beginning of a sequence of events that is leading us into more "uncharted territory".

When the number of people turning 60 years old (77 million Baby Boomers according to the U.S. Census Bureau were born between 1946 and 1964) begins to increase rapidly at the same time that the Gen X generation's much lower birth rate (49 million born between 1965 and 1976) collides with the quickly increasing numbers of retirement-aged Boomers, we (along with other developing countries) will find ourselves short tens of millions of qualified applicants on a daily basis. "So?" you say, "the Boomers need to work longer anyway."

Well, a person who is looking ahead strategically might ask these questions:

- Through 2025, who will be old enough and ready with the right kind of income and credit to afford large homes and family cars?
- Will there be enough people working in companies to occupy existing office buildings?
- Will the U.S. have enough "employable citizens": computer literate, sober, and trainable?
- Will there be enough workers to assume the work of 65-to-70 year olds in another five-to-ten years?
- What about Gen X? Are they a big enough demographic to pick up the slack?
- How many Boomers will opt to keep working full-time rather than part-time?
- What will happen to compensation rates if there is a frantic "financial survival" grab for all levels of talent?
- Will new automation and technology fill the gaps and if that happens, what types of traditional jobs will be left for Generation Y in 15 years?
- How many companies will be forced out of business for lack of available talent?
- What is the vision for addressing the financial survival of Boomers, Gen X and Gen Y?

Shortages are likely to become more dramatic as a majority of Boomers approach 70 years old. Gen X is a significantly smaller population than either the Boomers or Gen Y. This smaller group of able bodied, trainable/trained, mid-life workers will be "all there is" until the Gen Y group/Echo Boomers (born between 1984 and 2002) mature enough to fill in behind this much smaller labor pool.

As I republish this book at the end of 2015, we still have relatively high unemployment numbers, people losing their homes, others going into financial ruin, and many self-employed people without incoming business. Hundreds of thousands, if not millions, of college graduates are struggling financially...many unable to find jobs at all. But we can expect to see these dire circumstances flip-flop at some point.

At the same time that this is happening in the United States, half of Canada's government leadership will be eligible to retire. Japan will experience a negative birth rate that puts them at risk in very unique ways. Europe will have similar problems to the U.S. and Canada.

If you are thinking strategically, you may be wondering:

- What are the implications for salaries if most talent is in extreme demand?
- Is our government planning for any of this now or later?
- If Mexico and India are two of the countries that will not be affected by this demographic shift, are we ready for the implications of their availability?
- What are the implications for businesses that can't hold onto, or get enough bodies to keep their doors open? What will they do to get existing employees to stay?
- How will employees' attitudes change? Where will trust and engagement begin and end?
- What happens to strategic plans and the survival of businesses when there aren't enough doctors, technicians, call

center or hospitality staff? From where will our scientists, lab technicians, auto care and educational staff be recruited?

- How will computer literacy shortages be addressed as our nation turns to automation and self-service?
- Who will be available to lead? Are flatter, latticed organizations the future?
- How much regionalization and standardization will we see and can we expect it to affect us?

The truth of the matter is, that whether it's a "good" labor market or a "bad" economy, we tend to find excuses to not have a long range vision or plan, and just shoot from the hip. What's the advantage of having a Desired State for 2018 or 2020? How can we move towards our goals when they seem so far away and even impossible? How can we see the light at the end of the tunnel, adjust as we go, and enjoy the journey? Or will it be easier to fight fires for another decade until we can see where the chips fall (personally and professionally)? There's a famous saying: "If you don't know where you are going, you may end up some place else!" Wouldn't it be easier to participate in a global plan together?

The Role of Strategy

In a survival mode, it's very tempting to turn our backs on big picture thinking and having a strategy.

Why stop to create a desired state in the middle of chaos and survival? As Americans we struggle with focus and alignment because as a culture we like to solve problems and move quickly.

We also struggle with staying the course because we are perfectionists. If it doesn't happen exactly like we planned, then either someone beat us at it, or it must have been a bad idea. We need to learn how to stay focused on where we want to "be", how we want to "become" in the pursuit of our goals, and let the journey unfold. Perhaps we will get somewhere (that we want to be) FASTER because it didn't happen to unfold just as we had planned. In reality, successful changes don't happen predictably or sequentially... they unfold as they will or won't...but ideally, it's important to have an end result in mind when we start.

What is the end result in this case? "Maintaining our fiscal strength, profitability, keeping our market share, and being a company where employees want to work and customers want to buy." If we can't have it all, then maybe the goal becomes to survive by depending on each other's ingenuity and collaboration. Easy or hard, it's still better to go through hell and back with our values and dreams intact!

Beware of Short Term Solutions

Too many organizations go into cost cutting and layoffs as a reaction to tough times. You often hear: There is money to be saved right now! Cutting staff saves money and cutting our vendors' and suppliers' profits will help our bottom line.

Does short term planning have its value? Of course. But when there is a long term plan, the dream never goes away; it just gets temporarily diverted. It's still there through all the short-term wins and short-term solutions and disruptions. Rarely do we lose what is still there under all the layers of superficial changes. In the end we may have actually met the goal but lost track of the evidence.

Many times, it isn't packaged as we had thought it might be. Or we may forget to look to see how much headway we made while we were distracted. Often with a short-term solution, we cut off our leg to save money on shoes. You can't get your leg back later, and it's much less devastating to go without shoes temporarily.

When we don't think strategically, which means that we don't look outside of our own situation to see the bigger picture of what is actually going on...

- We miss important details.
- We dismiss the reality of our little and big successes.

- We miss the rich conversations and collaborations.
- We unnecessarily declare "failures".
- We miss our actual progress.

A true strategy can thrive in the middle of distracting changes or disruptions. It lives on like a tulip bulb in the ground...ready to emerge in its own time and to bloom victorious. Can you think of a time when you have ignored a success because it didn't appear how, where and when you had imagined it...but it was still there?

Case Study: The Multiple Planes of Existence

When I was in my late 20's I wanted to be a professional cartoonist. I worked hard to make it work, but other opportunities blocked my direction, and the only professional cartooning I did was for a few book authors who needed book covers. One person in particular loved my work. He traveled all over the world as a speaker on the topic of creative problem solving (Sid Parnes). For a very long time, I wondered about that phase of my life; I had tried so hard and wanted it so badly. Why hadn't I become a cartoonist; and not just any cartoonist, an internationally recognized one? About 10 years later, I was at an annual conference where Sid Parnes was teaching during the day. It was an after work breakout session, and I had a chance to meet some of the people who had been attending the daytime workshops. We were put into groups and my group was asked to go around in a circle introducing ourselves by name in preparation for an exercise that was coming. A man from Brazil was going to follow me after I introduced myself. When I said my name, he perked up and with big happy eyes yelled out, "Oh! You're the CARTOONIST in Sid's book! You are Timi...it's so exciting to meet you!"

It took me a second to register what he had just said to me! I was a bit dumbfounded, but he was right. Sid Parnes and his books (with my cartoon and cover designs) had been all over the world. And somehow this man knew my name and in his eyes, I only had

ONE IDENTITY. To him, I was that international cartoonist I wished that I could be. Then, just recently, another person who only knew me by my cartoons found me on Facebook and contacted me to see if I'd done any more cartoons lately. At this point, it's been well over thirty years! I had given up, but while I was focused on my lack of success, my cartoons were traveling to Africa, Holland, Europe, Scandinavia, and across the United States. It didn't turn out as I had imagined, but becoming an international cartoonist had definitely happened while I wasn't watching.

Case Study: An Invisible Business Transformation

At an all-day department offsite, I helped a 20-person marketing department set professional development goals for the year ahead. Their competitive climate was changing fast. They knew their professionalism and accountability had to advance quickly or they would be unable to keep up professionally in another year. It was a passionate discussion and they walked away that day excited and motivated. The team had even thrown in some extra credit work; they would reach out during the coming year to delight and better serve their internal customers and stakeholders. They were on fire! It seemed like it would be so easy, and one thing was sure, it was already "done" because they left aligned and excited that day. Now it was just a matter of time and focus.

However, after everyone returned to work, the following months were challenging. Budget cuts started; there wasn't time for follow up meetings. Everyone became very distracted. Then a program for early retirement was offered and two key players left. Next, a key person who had volunteered to help with financial and metric-related peer education left the company, and still another person was promoted out. Now, the department was spread very thin, trying to pick up the skillsets of four other people's jobs.

The first of the year brought more setbacks and surprises. A large corporate marketing investment was made to help the department produce competitive programming and promotions; this created even more work for them. We worried about them becoming burned out and demoralized. Now everyone was doing one and a half jobs and additionally rolling out a corporate-mandated initiative. Painfully, another eight months passed without a follow-up discussion about the exciting goals from last year's offsite.

Why It Didn't Matter

The year before, the new behaviors had been documented and had been emotionally internalized as a viable goal. We "were there" and all we had to do was implement and practice the new skillsets. The main focus had been to improve skill levels. The changes were largely related to increasing professional accountability in the areas of fiscal management, stronger collaboration, and increased demographic and segmented tracking.

As each employee took on new work and more work, they had to apply greater time management skills, work cross-functionally, and learn new content. In order to survive, they had to BECOME the goals they had set. With time, they saw their competitive muscle build and broaden but it seemed it was ONLY as a survival response. The professional gain and progress was being overlooked.

When we finally had a chance to meet up at a strategy session some 13 months later, we revisited the old levels of competence and examined the new skill sets to see how close they had gotten. It took the group a few minutes to ruminate about what still wasn't working smoothly before they realized that perfection was not the goal. Success rarely appears as a "still shot"; they would find themselves continuing to function in this highly dynamic environment for quite a while longer. In fact, it was possible that it might never stop.

As we talked about the skillsets that they had committed to learn, and the increased accountability that they had signed up for, it became gradually clear that the shift had occurred without ceremony. As we discussed the self-admitted gaps that were lingering from within their confidence, we started to hear from around the room, "We always do that now", "We have to do that or we couldn't survive this", "Oh that just comes naturally now…but it's not perfect yet."

Then the group started to articulate examples of how they weren't the same people they had been a year and a half earlier. Although their path had been crooked, and the expected steps had been delayed, all of the professional goals had been met, and in fact exceeded! Could they still get stronger and gain more control? "Yes!" But the necessary mindsets and new approaches had occurred as planned. The group was stunned!

Set the Course and Recalibrate as Needed: A One Step Plan to Accomplish Any Goal

It is my experience that you can get to any goal if you have "registered it emotionally":

- Whether or not you work the goal
- Whether or not conditions seem to have taken you completely off track
- Whether or not it occurs exactly the way you had hoped.

To "register it emotionally" means to:

- Desire it
- Be excited about it
- Be able to imagine completing it
- Be able to imagine what else is possible after you are finished

Our Future Is a Strategy

In the case of our demographic challenges and the changing economy and the U.S. labor market, what will we be able to imagine for our future? How will we be able to change and grow as we roll with the conditions and challenges that lie ahead? What can we imagine for ourselves and the shrinking middle class? Or do we want to take our chances?

Having a positive Desired State on your radar supports you to remain emotionally untangled during difficult delays. Because your vision is bigger than the delay, the promise of a passionate future helps you stay focused on a successful transition. To work without a strategy, you risk the chance of becoming psychologically demoralized from lack of structure and focus. It is hard to win without a well-rooted vision. Without a desired state to help you keep your focus, you can only problem solve and scramble. With a long term vision, you can work towards it and get back on track even when life pulls you off temporarily. We all need to have a way to measure what we have achieved. Our clearly written and emotionally anchored Desired State locks in our subconscious. It is that valuable long term strategic vision and accompanying metrics that see us through many personal sacrifices and add to our resilience during turbulent times. Businesses need heart too. And the ones who have passionate people driving results and innovation seem to have the best experience.

Setbacks are always bound to happen, digressions occur, and people and circumstances change, but a true strategy is just a "done deal" waiting to manifest in plain view.

We Quit Too Early

Why then do we quit? Time is money. Profits and egos rule. Wall Street scares us.

Several thought-provoking books that I recommend for learning more about "not giving up" and how (and why) to keep your focus are:

1. The Dip by Seth Grodin
2. Peaks and Valleys by Spencer Johnson
3. The Slight Edge by Jeff Olson.

4. <u>Political Dilemmas at Work: How to Maintain Your Integrity and Further Your Career</u> by by Ranker, Phipps, and Gautrey

Although eventually the economy or labor market will return to some kind of equilibrium, we cannot count on it returning to the way it was. So how do YOU want it to "be" as you go forward? If we refuse to stop and articulate a Desired State, or we never make sure we have a strategy, what can we expect to have after we emerge from the fray?

No Easy Answers

Yes, we can offshore and outsource to other countries and let immigrants do some of the jobs we cannot fill. But with the exceptions of India and Mexico, all other European, Canadian and Asian countries are going to experience their own simultaneous versions of this same low birthrate crisis. They all have their own shortages to contend with and each will have their own aging populations to manage. (Are you wondering how this low birth rate happened? It occurred during the 1960's in the first decade of the sexual revolution and with the mass availability of birth control.)

Do you know of any significant long range planning that is proactively addressing shortages of people and resources? If it will be affecting your employees, won't it also be impacting your customers? Can you expect your customer base to shrink? If not, have you looked at the age distribution of your customer base to see how it tracks? Are your vendors able to fill their jobs? How does this information potentially affect your industry? Would it make a difference to have planning conversations about these things? Would having a contingency plan for each potential scenario ease the experience?

Create a Desired State

Action Step One:

- Make sure you can imagine the feeling of accomplishment, the emotional rewards, the mental advantages, and freed-up time.
- Allow yourself to imagine the celebrations that follow any success you set out to accomplish.
- Apply your five senses to visualizing the future until you experience the hair on the back of your forearms tingle with clarity. When you have done those things and written down your Desired State with dates and sensory tags, you can be sure you have locked the experience into your consciousness.
- Visit your desired state periodically but at the very least, visit it on the day (or the year) that you set it, then again six months after the day you were scheduled to arrive. You will be amazed how much you have exceeded your own expectations just by being clear and emotionally anchored.

Inspire Yourself and Others

Ideally you'll read your Desired State several times a year and revisit the mental and physical excitement of wanting it and reaching your business dreams. Imagine the changes you want to make professionally and financially "done". But if you don't check your written vision, and you check it a year or two later, you will most likely find you've been successful anyway. That's how powerful your mind and heart are when they work together.

Inspire your employees with your vision and share your dream for a transformed department or company.

Action Step Two:

Keep your mind and heart open to other interpretations of the events that seem to be thwarting your efforts and dreams. Stay focused on the bigger picture and true significance of events. Look at your desired outcomes and ask yourself if you are shooting high enough. Make sure that your future is inspiring and worth the self-discipline and dedication to imagine it with your senses.

And remember: Disruptions and delays don't have to undermine your plans. From disruption we have seen many previously unpredicted opportunities.

There is a wonderful quote that goes something like this: *"May the bridges I burn light my way!"*

This can have several meanings: the most popular being that we need to learn from our mistakes. Another being, that the light shows us new paths, new opportunities, and sometimes the true direction of our journey.

* * *

NEXT: Is the political environment in your company holding you back?

Chapter 4:
The Fire Beneath the Surface— Internal Politics

"When We Don't See Systems We...

Fall out of the possibility of partnership with one another,
Misunderstand one another,
Make up stories about one another,
Have our myths and prejudices about one another,
Hurt and destroy one another,
Become antagonists when we could be collaborators,
Separate when we could remain together happily,
Become strangers when we could be friends,
Oppress one another when we could live in peace.

All of this happens without awareness or choice."

—Barry Oshry—SEEING SYSTEMS:
Unlocking the Mysteries of Organizational Life

IT'S OBVIOUS TO most people why a politically-charged working environment is undesirable, but how often do we factor in the subtle impact on our strategic goals? Why are we so reluctant to nip these undermining behaviors in the bud?

Negatively charged office politics get in the way of selling our creativity, our solutions, and expressing our engagement. In fact, runaway office politics work against increasing engagement. And the awful truth is that when teammates and leaders aren't aligned on their goals, aren't talking, and aren't brainstorming as one mind, they aren't going to meet their goals and realize their business plans.

It's very common to see one department "save" all the others fiscally. It's also very common for functional groups to work in silos all year and later to finger-point at "laggards" as the year-end results are reported.

Can you think of examples when you have witnessed this dynamic? Had you understood the root cause, how might you have approached meeting your goals differently? At the time, if you had a better idea of the subtle devastation going on underneath the surface of day-to-day operations, could you have potentially addressed it?

But I'm Only One Person

Not only are you "only one person", but you are most likely a manager who is not calling the shots and is running everything alone. You are like David against Goliath's army – outnumbered. But speaking of "shots", what did David do? He took a shot at it and artfully took care of the problem. That is why this chapter could be useful to you. Many of the problems we have can be predicted and then addressed with a systematic approach.

Office Politics Work against Our Success

The political climate of a company is important to everyone's success. How healthy the climate is turns out to be significant for BOTH the game players and the people who hate it. More often than not, the people who hate politics try to ignore what is going on. It's a losing approach even though in the short term, it's a relief to be ignorant of the daily emotional roller coaster; a political environment needs to be managed.

The people who are engaged in political games, may be finding short term relief in their successes, but their failures and thwarted efforts take a toll on their health and attitude. Everyone involved is dragged into the undertow of negative office politics. The stress that results can ruin morale and weaken team alignment. And it can seem insidious.

Office politics are born from fear. Fear of losing. Fear of being abandoned. Fear of being criticized or embarrassed. In severe cases it's also fear of not being at the top of the pile. Understanding how unproductive political games start and what some possible interventions might be, can improve your "strategic partner" status.

Be An Opportunist

Since it's likely that the shifting economy and evolving labor market will continue to wreak havoc on our work lives for years to come, lots of new stress is going to come our way. It's very important to partner with your boss and other key employees during difficult times to find ways to reduce stress.

Hopefully you don't work in a company where politics are severe. And although you may know some people who thrive on playing political games, most people do not want negative office politics anywhere near them. That being said, ignoring office game playing doesn't usually work.

Politics Can Make or Break Your Career

The problem is that politics at work (and the quality of the relationships that ensue) can hamper your career success. If you don't understand why, just think about the rules of engagement on the TV show "Survivor" or any of the other competitive reality shows where contestants are vying for a job, their own show, or a chance to win a million dollars. On a daily basis, we are seeing average people sabotage each other without consequence. It becomes one of the ugly truths about human nature, and we begin to accept this dishonest behavior as "normal".

Negative Politics is a Stress Behavior

There is nothing "normal" about office politics. It is born out of stress responses to real or perceived circumstances.

Stress responses keep us down into the trenches and keep us focused on firefighting. For success to occur, we need to be aligned around executing strategy…not grappling on a daily basis (or hourly basis!) with tactical problems that force us into the weeds. Politics begets pettiness.

Teammates Shouldn't Be Your Competition

Outsiders are the competition. They wreak havoc by changing their pricing, attacking us via the media, or lying about their services and products. Outsiders are our commercial affiliates with different cultures. Outsiders are vendors with sub-standard customer service. Outsiders are governmental agencies. The list is endless. Outsiders are NOT our coworkers.

Political dysfunction can become impossibly complicated for you when you begin to consider how to become a better partner. "Whom to trust" and "which situations to trust" are at the core of betrayals. Figuring out how to navigate your way through these issues requires extra work.

You may want to read the books: The Five Dysfunctions of a Team and Silos, Politics and Turf Wars by Patrick Lencioni, and Leadership and Self Deception: Getting Outside the Box by the Arbinger Institute. All are written as business novels and lay out their principles metaphorically. High adventure and real life drama play out vividly in the real world of business.

Making Distinctions

It is important to be able to spot specific business environments that tend to make a political climate likely. These are environments where job insecurity and fear abound. How many do you recognize?

1. **Unprofitable periods:** the pressure is on to bring in results! Staff and their managers are targets for job loss if financial goals are not met. Watch for corruption or manipulation of people, numbers and sales.
2. **Highly Profitable periods:** do you see spending issues? Are there empires being built? Is there evidence of envy or arrogant behavior? Do you see competition between departments for operating budget?
3. **Tight** markets: when there is a tight budget except for very important projects (usually sales and marketing efforts or pet projects), watch for more of the behaviors in 1 and 2.
4. **Pre-sale** times when no one realizes the company may change ownership and all decision-making stops…insecurity and confusion set in and "speculation" escalates.
5. During a potential sale that is **public knowledge:** fear and uncertainty ignite the worrying, gossip and speculation that detour us from our goals.
6. **Threats to the privacy and security of others:** intimate affairs or conflict of interest relationships pose a threat to team work and trust that is hard to nail down. No matter how discreet a couple is "the perception of" is always going to be disruptive. When immediate family, best friends, old cronies, and lovers are discovered, insecurity and fantasy set in. Fraternizing at work and the creation of ambiguous work relationships creates insecurity because of unclear boundaries. Those on the outside looking in become threatened. I find this one to be a highly under-rated issue…especially by those involved.

7. **Government funded projects:** where funding could be lost due to a change in priorities by Congress or the state governments. Who will be the first to go?

8. Highly **unsophisticated businesses:** You see this most often. When the inexperienced or unsophisticated leaders of a small company (privately or publicly held) run daily operations, unaware of (or disinterested in) sound business practices and straightforward, businesslike leadership. Their poor attitudes result in behaviors towards customers, employees, and vendors that breach trust and sound business practices. Micromanaging, backstabbing, under-managing, and weak leadership are the daily fare. Frustration and demoralization set in. Insecurity is high, and the incidence of law suits (or threats of them) starts to escalate.

9. **Any changes in leadership** to the group can trigger insecurities in the people who remain. Are they next? Who will act as their political cover? Changes in vision, culture and/or philosophy are stressful to survivors. Who will be the next to go?

Neutralizing Hot Spots

How is it an advantage to you as a coach, HR professional or functional leader to be able to spot these situations? Do you have the necessary partnerships to turn these lumps of coal into gold?

- Can you dispel the rumors or coach others on how to handle the gossip?
- Can you introduce communication and educational topics that will inspire others?
- Can you help articulate and set "a new direction" as changes occur?
- Can you resist the temptations to hire "your own kind" by following best practices?
- Are you willing to refuse to hire relatives if they will be placed in compromising situations?

- Are you willing to speak up against fraternizing at work? Are you willing to hold the line with those who see themselves as the exception to every rule?
- And most importantly, how do you avoid getting into these highly charged situations? What are some new screening techniques you can apply to your job search that will begin to minimize the odds that you will seek employment with a politically charged company in the first place?

When we work in a company that is business-like and is practicing sound business practices, a person who strives to be a strategic business partner is most likely to be appreciated and understood.

- Does your company openly share its goals?
- Is there a strategic plan (future state) in addition to an operating plan (budget and business initiatives)?
- Will you (or your internal clients) have the professional opportunity to contribute ideas that are politically attractive to the management team?
- Will you be working with coworkers who are experiencing job satisfaction and daily success?

Companies in Transition

Sometimes, we accept positions in companies that are in (or just coming out of) some big business transition. Perhaps they have just been sold, become publicly held, or are experiencing new leadership. There may be vague goals around culture, around their new market, or around sales strategies. Ideally, it shouldn't be that way, but that's what happens. Long range planning may have been short circuited due to impatience to firefight. And sometimes inexperience and indecision can hold up progress.

In this case, long term strategies may seem difficult to set and it's easier to develop goals that focus around short-term solutions— short term solutions that show quick and measurable results. But at the same time, you will want to address alignment behind the company's long term goals as soon as possible. In transition, the key is to take daily or weekly steps towards a long range vision, no matter how far off it is.

Consider Who You Are Aligned with and Why

Stories about real-life corporations like Enron, WorldCom, or the late-great Arthur Anderson Consulting and some of our most popular Hollywood movies contribute to our reluctance to trust (and fear of being tricked by) teammates. It's possible to proactively manage the root cause of political behaviors and insecurities when you understand them better. As a strategic partner, you can potentially neutralize many emotionally charged work situations. The most important thing to remember is that you can't expect to conquer these big issues alone.

Finding Your Master Mind Group

I could have called this your "support group" but why not think about this more dynamically? These are the people with whom you need to be aligned, engaged with, and who will participate with you in achieving your goals and crafting your Desired State. Your master mind group:

- Will fuel and appreciate your efforts and strategic perspective.
- Will have a similar approach to bridging the gap between Current and Desired State.
- Will be easiest to partner with.
- Will form alliances with you and become more than coworkers.

Assess Your Partnerships

Learn other people's personality quirks and be clear about your own. We ALL have quirks! If you aren't sure what yours are, take a

Birkman or Myers Briggs assessment and be sure to take the time to get to know more about your team members' lives and families, outside of your professional lives. Yes, you'll get to know them better as you work together, but in a crisis, you will have to have developed rapport ahead of time. Take the time to do that before you need to cash in during a crisis.

Case Study: The Survival Game

Once I was at a retreat with my CEO at our company headquarters. We were with 24 other movers and shakers within our global organization. The facilitators gave us a game to play and put us on opposite teams with minimal resources and a very stressful timeline. Both sides immediately became locked in a struggle to win.

It seemed that no one could win if we didn't collaborate. Each team was short of resources. You could hear the tremendous amount of heckling and competitive behavior as it began to fill up the room. Both sides were losing.

As I watched things unfold, I noticed there was a lot of fear in the room and that the facilitators were saying and doing intimidating things to heighten that fear. We were all on our feet on either side of a taped off middle section. The room was huge. Some of our bravest and more athletic were trying to forge their way across this area of pitfalls in the middle. At the right time (I say that because "moments earlier" might not have been long enough) I asked my team if they were willing to collaborate with the other team if I could get my CEO to talk to his side about collaborating with us. I also addressed the issue of cheating to win; everyone would HAVE to agree not to cheat. Would they agree to play cooperatively if I could get him to promise that his team would agree not to cheat to win either? In a very short time, I was able to get both sides to agree to collaborate. We completed the assignments and were able to finish the game very shortly after that. Both teams had won. They had timed us. We succeeded because we had decided to collaborate and acted with integrity within that agreement. What we had been DO-ing wasn't going to work. What we BE-came once we put our heads together, sealed the deal.

What Made Us Ready to Partner?

At dinner that night, the groups were acknowledged and my boss and I were awarded the "Strategic Network" award. As it turned out, both teams received credit for completing the game in record time. How had this occurred?

- After struggling and failing repeatedly, we began to see that we couldn't win with the limited resources that we had.
- We knew we needed additional resources and brain power.
- We saw an advantage in using a trustworthy resource.
- The other team was looking for more options, too.
- My boss was intrigued with my assertiveness and proposal.
- He trusted me, and my team trusted the rapport and confidence that I had with my CEO.
- We decided to "take a chance" and thankfully, we were all accountable and trustworthy.
- There were no shenanigans. People on both sides chose to keep "their word". It was risky; because anyone from either team could have left the other team demoralized.
- We had to give up tactical thinking and we had to give up competing for designing a joint end game.

How Does One Become More Adept at Reducing Political Games?

The obvious answer is, don't hire politically charged people.

- Hire people with reputations for good integrity and collaborative personalities.

- Create stability by figuring out what other people need to perform at their best.
- Anticipate their potential objections, and determine how you can "delight them".
- Get to know your teammates and stakeholders.
- If you can't figure out how they think and what they need, ask someone who knows them better to help you figure out where to start. This is especially important if you are to become a credible "strategic partner" yourself.

How Do You Develop Credibility?

- Figure out your own influencing style (Influencing for Results assessment)
- Figure out your coworkers' influencing style; how can you address their unspoken needs?
- Become familiar with your own and their stress behaviors and foibles.
- Show an interest in the stress response of teammates and help them when they are in stress or are headed down a risky path.
- Be courageous with your observations and insights when strategy is lacking (see the book Crucial Conversations)
- Partner with all people equally and respectfully. Whether it's your boss or his second-in-command, or the custodian. Everybody counts.
- Remember you are always being judged by others, whether you are on stage or off. People already have an impression of you (fair or not) before you propose an idea.

Keeping Your Head Out of the Sand

You don't have to be a politician, but you *do* have to be politically savvy. To NOT admit that certain people can ruin or advance your career...and squash your good ideas...is professionally naïve.

Learn who pulls the strings around the office. Learn who is working for positive change, and who is not. Reach out to others to craft a desired future for behavior, for the health of the culture, and for the good of the company.

When you manage politics in every area of your life, it will feel more natural to master it at work.

Who Has The Ball Politically?

Here are some guidelines for figuring out who's pulling the strings (good or bad). Look to see who...

- controls the purse strings and controls the budgets.
- has the boss's ear *(who is in the CEO's office the most?)*.
- is bringing in the sales.
- is working on the high profile projects.
- is finding ways to reduce and control operating expenses.
- is managing their departments with the fewest employee problems.

Attributes of a Strategic Partner:

1. Helping to create initiatives that show understanding of long term and high level goals.
2. Suggesting ways to decrease losses and reduce operating costs.
3. Showing how to measure results and transform those results into a track record.
4. Assuring that results are easy to understand and a "quick high-level read".
5. Making sure that all proposals and conversations reflect the company's goals and budgetary constraints even in good times.

6. Presenting one's "self" (dress, language, timing, choices) appropriately and professionally to each situation and opportunity
7. Being willing to initiate critical conversations with key stakeholders when it is not popular to create waves or may feel intimidating to you.

Building Your Reputation As a Strategic Partner

When you can make others look good by creating results for them, you will be sought after as a partner and advisor again and again. People who make good choices **are not** a dime a dozen.

Although you can't afford to be in the game by yourself, not everyone will share this point of view and you may not have much moral support at times. A strong person may occasionally have to bear the brunt of success or failure. That being said: don't hesitate to upgrade your supporters and teammates as appropriate. If you are in with a weak crowd, go looking for a stronger bunch. You deserve it. You'll be assessed by your team, and it's easier to think strategically when you have others around you.

Case Study: Unintentional Politics

Once, we were going through a lay off at work. It was well-orchestrated and many of the affected employees had opportunities to apply for other positions. I was on a team of people who were processing and assisting the employees. One of my assignments was to act as an advisor to a department who had 12 affected employees and another eight job openings that they could fill. Our HR Department was working around the clock to track daily progress with screenings, interviews, number of jobs applied for, and results of interviews. Eventually, they would be ready to track the number of job offers; but not everyone had been fully screened and not everyone had finished interviewing the internal candidates. There was a possibility that a displaced employee who interviewed well could land multiple job offers.

Before any offers were made, the plan was to debrief the candidate on each potential offer and help them prioritize them. We wanted them to be fully aware of their choices. We also wanted to be able to size up what might happen to some employees who weren't as likely to get offers. We didn't want them to see jobs closing before they were given an opportunity to be debriefed. So, it was important that efforts were carefully coordinated and that everyone, from the top down, was in lockstep coordination.

One department head was barging forward with great enthusiasm and competitive aplomb. She was mentally about two to three days ahead of our plan of action and wanted to be "the first" to make offers so that "her people" could have jobs before the end of the week! Despite attempts to slow down the process and explain the correct HR procedures to this leader and her team, an offer was made without including HR. It was hurtful to the HR team.

- It was done without the knowledge or involvement of HR (not part of the agreement)
- It did not take into account any other potential offers that might be available to the employee.
- Laying in the wake of this successful job offer was one very devastated and embarrassed HR Generalist who was now going to have to explain to her boss how she had failed to follow proper procedure.
- There were fair employment practice liabilities (what if a candidate was given preferential treatment or if a candidate found out later that they had not received full disclosure of all the available job opportunities?)
- It "appeared" that the HR Generalist did not have the respect of the department head and her middle manager who had made the offer.

What's the Best Way to Resolve a Mess?

First, I visited the hiring manager because he seemed to be the guilty party.

Of course, what I found was that he'd been put in a (seemingly) "do or die" situation with his boss who had ordered that the job offer be made.

He had gotten caught between his boss' orders and the protocol the HR Business Partner had been given.

Both choices were no-win and he had been put on a deadline. The hiring manager reluctantly went with his boss' wishes and deeply hurt his relationship with his HR business partner.

At 6:00 p.m. at night, I headed for the big boss' office. The hiring manager advised me NOT to go through with any kind of confrontation. The big boss was there in her office. She was a tough one. I took a deep breath (maybe my last), requested permission to ask some questions, and laid out my concerns:

1. Did she believe in the Accountability Training that we were all taking? *Yes.*
2. Did she understand that true accountability unites us as inter-dependent on each other for success? *Yes.*
3. Had the Human Resource Department "stepped up"? Were they doing a terrific job? *Yes.*
4. Had she ever seen the HR Department be as professional or work so hard? *No! They were terrific.*
5. Would it bother her if the HR Department stumbled and fell because someone compromised their efforts or because of moving too fast, someone made it look like they were not doing excellent work? (hesitation...point hit home) *I'll think about it...OK, you can leave now!*

I left sure that someone besides me would NOT sleep well that night.

The next day at the daily check-in meeting, it was clear that the problem had been fixed, and I could tell that it wouldn't happen again! There were new instructions and a new approach that was 180 degrees from the day before.

But what happened much later is the real moral of the story...

I never told the head of HR about my concerns about the other department leader. I didn't need to; everything was obviously fixed. And I never went back to the hiring manager nor did he approach me. I saw the bad situation completely self-correct the next day and was satisfied with the result. It seemed like someone had gotten to the HR Generalist too. The incident was never mentioned again.

But two months later, the head of HR told me that the other department head had immediately come to him to apologize! Apologize?! I had overlooked something.

I had not given the "peer sabotage" issue any consideration at all. But of course, if the errant department head had brought down the morale of all the HR generalists (because each of them risked being treated the same way by other trigger happy groups) and the public reputation of the HR Department during such an emotional time was damaged, additionally (and this is the part I had overlooked) it would unintentionally be a professional blow to the reputation of the leader of HR, too.

The other leader had realized this and "confessed" her poor behavior and apologized before any further damage could be done. Do you think there was trust built that day? Now I knew what had caused the HR Generalist to calm down and why the hiring manager never asked me about it again. Everyone was made whole and was fully satisfied.

The boss had come down the very next morning (very early) and had apologized for putting the hiring manager into a compromising situation and for damaging his reputation with HR. She had also personally apologized to the HR Generalist on behalf of them both! No wonder everyone was so "over it"!

I was thanked for being a true strategic partner and for being fearless! Although I hadn't been without fear, I had done "the hard thing". I have to say that my efforts produced some unexpected results. That is often the way it works. It's these moments that keep us coming back to do it again and again. Here's what I experienced:

- Mutual respect was re-established and powerfully affirmed
- Confidence was restored
- Integrity was locked in for the future
- Rapport was strengthened
- A desire to "team up again" lingers in our memories as a result of this self-correction
- Success occurred in resolving differences of opinion and style

When we are all connected, any little thing we do to politically hurt a team mate affects all of us.

In Summary

To become a strategic partner in a politically healthy work-place, regard others as your teammates and seek out ways to work together. Start with controlling your own insecurities. Learn about yourself and become emotionally intelligent. Get out of unhealthy situations if they can't be improved. Remember that your ideas and contributions are only as valuable as the people who use them.

Learn to collaborate with other managers so they can show in their progress reports that they worked with you to complete their goals. Show in your progress reports that you worked with others to attain mutual goals. Emphasize partnership and idea sharing. To be able to partner like that is to harness the true power of collaboration and keep it elevated above office politics. It is also a way to become very popular and valuable to *any* team.

Do You Behave This Way? A Checklist

- Demonstrate that you are effective by being prepared and thorough in your presentations and proposals.

- Avoid being perceived as privately or publicly biased towards any coworkers or vendors.
- Behave and present yourself in a business-like and strategic manner with everyone. Be honest and straightforward in all **your communications.**
- **Don't assume that just because someone else talks like an** idea was theirs, that any one else is thinking that is was. On the other side of that, practice *smart trust*: communicate your ideas to the right people and keep your superiors informed regularly.
- Speak up gently and appropriately to coworkers who start to "go political".
- Work at the root cause of political problems to alleviate worry and lack of communication that will fuel politics.

* * *

NEXT: How do you help tactical thinkers become more strategic?

Chapter 5:
Convincing Tactical Thinkers to "Go Strategic"

*"Motivation is the art
of getting people to do
what you want them to do
because they want to do it."*

—Dwight D. Eisenhower

IT'S VERY HARD to partner with someone strategically if they are (or you are) confused about what strategic behavior is. Be prepared for MOST people to confuse "a strategy" with an action step. An action step is something you DO. A strategy is how **you (or your company) are going to BE in the process of executing action steps. In the last chapter we talked about being strategic** rather than being political. BEING is how you think. DOING are the action steps you take.

Be alert for confusion and keep in mind that your success as a Strategic Partner depends on how aligned you and your boss are on goals, strategy, and implementation. If either of you misunderstands the alignment that exists (or doesn't) between you, neither of you will get what you want.

Right now, you may see your role as someone who executes strategy, when really what you are doing is executing action steps. The strategy is usually something that triggers a long term shift in behavior, culture, or success. Weight Management may be a long term strategy for improving your health problems. What you DO to lose or gain weight are your actions. Exercising regularly, eliminating high fat foods, or drinking eight glasses of water are action steps.

Work towards alignment by discussing your mutual goals and your mutual approach. Then be prepared to speak up, look for opportunities, and to fully participate in being an accountability partner. Understanding HOW to speak up will be our next discussion, but before we move on, here are some work related examples regarding the difference between strategy (being) and action (doing).

Examples of Strategy at Work

1. Capturing market share is the STRATEGY. Notice that a strategy is generally broad reaching, purposefully vague, and may sound inspiring. It may utilize verbs that sound metaphorical. "Capture" is such a verb. What kinds of verbs does your company use?

The tactical ACTION STEPS supporting the strategy might be to:

- price products competitively.
- increase media advertising by 40% to raise brand awareness.
- sell 20% more services/products over last year.
- provide exceptional customer service.
- design a customer retention program

2. Improve Employee Engagement is the STRATEGY.
   The tactical ACTION STEPS are:

- Invite the employees to participate in changes and plans that require their ideas and cooperation
- Set clear metrics and milestones to help employees measure productivity.
- Provide training in change management and offer employee development opportunities.
- Provide training for the supervisors to show them how to praise and coach more effectively

Leader Perspectives and Audiences

Your ability to understand and appreciate the unique needs of the various functional groups, and within those groups, the various priorities at each level of the organization, will solidify your role as a strategic partner. A common error in partnering is to not realize the various perspectives of leaders. We lump supervisors, managers and top management into a "leadership group" which limits our ability to persuade and gain support at the different levels.

Additionally, the further down on the hierarchy, the more tactical the lives of the leaders will be. Learn to adjust your own point of view to each leader's point of view. Consider what their role is and how easy it's going to be for them to engage in strategic thinking. Adjust your communication as needed.

The following is a potential way to distinguish between the perspectives of your leaders. Let's assume that you are recommending a way to increase employee engagement by rolling out a new program that teaches employees how to identify and use their transferable skills to improve their career mobility within your organization. Notice how each stakeholder group brings their own unique perspective to the evaluation process. Their priorities are not the same.

Points of View:

- Human Resources: "This program HAS to address the needs of all my stakeholders (the entire organization) and satisfy everyone's viewpoint, or I haven't got time to do this! It sounds like it will empower the employees to identify their strengths and weaknesses and will turn this task (that I have little time to devote myself to) into a self-help tool that will help employees at all levels target other jobs within the company." (tactical)
- Employees: "Here's my chance for learning more about other jobs. Maybe I can qualify for a promotion which will address my needs for upward mobility". (tactical)
- Supervisors: "Here's a possible solution to my immediate problems with motivating and retaining talent around career progression. This might also help me increase my department's Employee Opinion Survey scores." (tactical)
- Middle Managers: "Is this program a "tool" that will integrate with key human resources functions like EEO, affirmative action, training, organizational development systems, performance management? It HAS to, or I haven't got time for this." (tactical)
- Top Managers: "If we fund this initiative will it give us the tools and data my leaders are missing? If it will help me identify leadership potential and create successors for the future, then I'm interested. Will it help me so that the next time I'm

asked about succession planning, I can show that I have my people identified? (strategic need that is stated tactically)

To consider these different stakeholder perspectives and to be able to discuss ideas with your boss and stakeholders from their unique points of view is one way to demonstrate your knowledge and the distinctions you are able to make in a business setting.

You can also use these viewpoints as criteria for assessing the feasibility of other peoples' initiatives.

Can you expect to meet the needs of all the groups? Find out by interviewing your stakeholders one-on-one (by survey and in person). Do these distinctions accurately reflect the needs within your company?

Common Roadblocks

As a strategic partner, you can't assume that the leaders you work with actually have the words for what they want and need. They should, but so often they humbly will admit that they don't. And as you saw previously, they don't always think and talk strategically, even though we think they should. I know many of you will be surprised by what I'm saying next, but if you don't assume their strategic superiority going in, the data and opinions you collect will be richer, more useable, and contain more new information than you ever expected to get.

In many instances, your supervisors and managers will only have a vague idea of what they want and may still be working to articulate segments of their role. It's fairly common to see this, and it stems from the mindset of believing you'll "know it when you see it." What seems like a perfectly obvious and simple question is sometimes to be met with "Wow, that's a GREAT question! I've never thought about it quite that way." So watch out for idealizing your leaders. They are just people too. They need and want your insights to bounce off their ideas.

When working with bosses, other leaders, and establishing yourself as a strategic partner, avoid overuse of buzz words; talking in the latest "business speak"; or appearing to come across academically fluent unless that's the culture of your company. It's not smart to intimidate your boss! Since you want the data you collect to be honest, exploratory, and measurable, you will want to set a comfortable tone. The more formal your approach and language, the more careful your audience will be. And odds are, they need someone they can let down their hair with and trust, so you don't want to make them feel uptight.

Set the comfort level; ask questions so they can be the ones doing all the talking, and let them be the ones to have a chance to be impressive (rather than it being you). Put people at ease and build rapport; they will appreciate you for it.

Chances are they've not had an opportunity to articulate their thoughts and feelings about strategy and the future. Approach this task with generosity. Be their safe harbor for exploration and finding their words. Ask good questions and be an exceptional listener; repeat what you hear to lock in understanding. Good questions are simple and logical, and usually aren't academic nor do they sound like a business school exam.

Questions that lead us away from stuck thinking and tactical solutions:

- What is the outcome you hope to create from this decision?
- What becomes possible after this phase and once you have met your goals?
- What were the events that lead you to this decision? Why were they important?
- Do you see any red flags along the way?
- Does it matter to you what the employees think and feel once they hear about your decision?
- What do you want people to say and feel after the event is over?

- Do you think that she is doing this with full awareness of how her behavior is being perceived? Or how it is impacting her team?
- Do you want to reinvent the outcome of this situation?
- How do you think consumers will perceive this?
- If we move forward quickly, who might object?
- What will stop you from succeeding? Whose help do you need?

Don't assume anything. One of the biggest misconceptions about leadership that I hear all the time is: "Well, you'd think if he/she got this far, they'd KNOW that!" It just doesn't work that way.

It's Lonely at the Top

In some organizations, there's a tendency to ridicule or demean leaders who openly admit that they don't have all the answers. I think it's a mistake to expect perfection. Leaders are our internal customers. It can be very lonely at the top, and as shocking as it may sound, MOST leaders do not have strong foundations. Frequently, they have not been adequately mentored or coached along the way; they have done their best and succeeded. They may not know exactly what they want, and they may feel afraid of being seen as a fraud. Haven't we all felt that way at some time?

Perhaps they have lots of formal training, but haven't had much time to integrate the lessons. As strategic partners, we have the opportunity to be a safe harbor for other people's ideas. Partner with them to explore outcomes and to learn to think and plan strategically together. Do this for your coworkers, too.

Make a Difference

Value is relative and it's subjective. How can you make a difference in your boss' life? Providing clarification and alignment is another key area where you can build a reputation as an extremely valuable strategic partner. Be approachable and in most cases, they will approach.

If you have ever read the book The Man Who Listens to Horses by Monty Roberts, you know the horse whispering technique already. Approachability was dramatically illustrated in the book when Roberts was able to build trust with the local deer around his house, in the same way he calmed and built trust with frightened horses.

Use a "coach approach" to ask good questions and to bring out the genius of others. Make it your job to provide that service. Use your Servant Leadership skills. Leaders can become intimidated just as easily as you can. Work to be approachable, confident and safe. I'm not talking about "dumbing down", but about being genuine and approachable in a powerful, professional way. Perhaps, you know someone who does that already? How can you become a student of their masterful style and effectiveness?

Promote Trust

Help your leaders and stakeholders to articulate and discuss their values, concerns and needs with you. You will be surprised by their trust and they will LOVE you for it. Never talk behind their back. Keep the environment safe for them and NEVER complain to someone else about their lack of knowledge or clarity…help your boss (and the other leaders that you come in contact with) to evolve and grow. Give the gift of leadership to others.

Your support will add tremendous strategic value, and because you will always be "one of the few" who could help them, your professional support will be valued for life. And as they grow professionally, so will you.

Being Willing to Be Strategic Despite the Pressures

Your simple structure and clear approach will set the stage for strategic conversations versus tactical ones. However, in some situations it will be difficult for you to be influential. Even so, you will need to demonstrate your courage by offering your point of view. Just go on record. No blurting or forcing. "Gosh, I see this so differently. We have opportunity in front of us... (wait for some curiosity)...this is how I see it"...then explain what you see.

It's guaranteed that down the road you will be approached by someone who wouldn't listen, but circled back later, to say: "You were right; I couldn't see it." They will do this because you remained approachable and patient with them. You didn't doubt your insights, and you didn't embarrass them, and you quietly stood your ground. When tactical people won't or can't seem to join you in becoming more strategic, smile and joke with them about the tension the discussion is causing. Patiently move on, because (you know) they aren't "ready" to let go of their non-strategic view point yet.

Stay open to the idea that your boss may not know anything about being strategic. He or she may know less about it than you do. Sometimes it will be lonely at the top for you!

Confident Things to Say When You Are in a No-Win Situation

Example 1:

"Ok, I can see I'm outnumbered on this one. But someday we are going to have to start doing the right thing, so it will be coming up again, but for now, I'll back off. You can have this win."

Be sure to flash a very BIG smile and look at EACH one of them. Be prepared for smirks, smiles with lowered eyes, and amazed looks. You have just turned a whole bunch of people into your biggest fans.

Example 2:

"I'm going to have to go on record as disagreeing with your perspective on this; I think we need to revisit this hot topic some other time and see if we can't find alignment in the future. In the interest of time, <u>I thank you for considering my point of view</u> and when you're ready, I'm ready to move on, too!"

Most likely you will get respectful and highly relieved "thank you's." Guaranteed, they will NOT be able to forget your elegant, confident concession.

The fact that they will not be able to forget what you did will spur many of them to involuntarily keep thinking about it until they can resolve it. This will of course, help you seal the deal next time.

Do you want to ask me, "What do I say next time?" It's highly likely that you will never have to bring it up again…it may resolve itself during the incubation period that follows your last interaction. They just needed time to think about it longer and make it their own decision. You have already won.

Develop Your Own Style and Voice

- Find your own voice and words as you consider these options. Are you ready to be this assertive and behave this confidently in front of others? Do you even want to take this responsibility? Strategic thinking is not the norm. It takes guts to speak up. Tactical thinking (or problem solving) is 99% of conversation. Just imagine the competitive edge any company has if they are ready to act strategically!

- Be careful about your tone of voice and speak medium-soft or adapt V-40 in your approach. V-40 is when you speak at 40% of your usual loudness. It is a powerful way to get others to take you seriously, or at the very least, to listen closely to your ideas.

- Do you notice implied strategic outcomes when people say that they are: "doing the right thing", "creating future alignment", "working this out"?

As a strategic partner, there's great magic in letting others "win". It's an art form to be able to reduce the struggle so that another person can think about what you said under less threatening conditions.

It takes a lot of confidence to let others save face at your expense. We often joke about "just make him or her think it was their idea and then they'll do whatever you want."

Many people react in ways that they don't understand any better than we understand them. If you are one of those people, I recommend that you consider taking a Birkman assessment; it's likely you will find the behavioral answers there.

Always stay engaged with a person socially enough to give them the opportunity to self-correct and save face. What's the goal anyway? Not "winning" but "right action" regarding strategy.

Be Patient and Generous

- Remember to give yourself time to build a reputation as credible and strategic.
- Give others time to reflect on your observations. Patience!
- Give others time to observe your accuracy and use of intuition at work.
- Give others time to increase their readiness to change and learn.
- Be generous with your patience when others are emotionally stuck.
- Assume positive intent when others respond back poorly; try to under-react and to give them time and leeway to self-correct (and possibly apologize).
- Learn how to predict when there will be a positive outcome despite a negative response.

Reframe your ability to "judge others" and have it mean that you know how to accurately predict positive outcomes and facilitate win-win solutions. Drop any negative connotation or behavior around judging.

Let the stressful responses you encounter from client groups play out without any retaliation. Ultimately, you will see difficult or defensive obstacles begin to melt away.

The truth usually rings true in people's hearts...trust that.

With time and experience, you will see your new ability to persuade and influence others become easier and extremely rewarding. A person who can think strategically has a valuable talent.

*   *   *

NEXT: Let's examine how smart timing and a company's life cycle phase can help us determine successful business strategy.

Chapter 6:
Being in the Right Place at the Right Time

"A company is not limited to linear cycles of growth like humans where aging eventually leads to death. A company can be revitalized through intentional "renewal". Understanding this leads to strategic sophistication."

—William Bridges

THIS IS ONE of those topics that may have a delayed reaction for many of you. It has a lot to do with successful strategy but it comes from uncommon thought. It is information to keep in mind as your career unfolds, and for some of you who are miserable in your current job, this may shed some light on why you feel miserable. It has to do with being in the right place at the right time and matching your strategy to your company's (or a potential company's) life cycle phase.

Just like living beings, companies have life phases. We can all see the difference between being in a start-up company versus being in a more established company. But, beyond that, we probably don't have much academic distinction. So, next we are going to call out some distinctions about the different phases that a company goes through as it grows and how that affects implementing and selecting appropriate strategy.

Just so you know, this is knowledge that once you have it, is fairly black and white. Once you use it, the process that follows doesn't require you to know anything else more about it. But from my perspective, if you don't have the information at all, then you might be stuck in "a grey area" for years. So this is why I'm dedicating a chapter to understanding (and being able to assess) a company's life cycle and how it can affect your ability to partner successfully.

First let me explain that much of the academic content of this chapter comes from the work of William Bridges, transition expert and guru on successful organizational change (http://www.wmbridges.com). This particular information is taken from his book titled: The Character of Organizations. You can also find it in his book, Managing Transitions.

When I first started working with this information about company life cycle issues, I used it to illustrate the fact that most of us gravitate to a "type of company" that works best for us. Without realizing it, we are gravitating to a particular life cycle phase and consequently, a certain strategic mind set.

In a group of experienced HR leaders, I had each person write down:

1. The names of the last five or more companies where you worked.
2. How long were you employed there?
3. Did you enjoy your position or was it a struggle?
4. Did you feel valued or misunderstood while you were there?
5. Which were their top 1 or 2 favorite companies and why?

I suggest you do this also, before you read on. (I'll wait while you do this little exercise for yourself ☺) Try to complete it in two minutes. This is not a test and no one will see your answers. (I'll go get a drink of water while you write)....

Life Cycles

Experts like Bridges have found that like the stock market, or the seasons, companies go through stages and phases. By understanding the life cycles of businesses, strategic thinkers can more accurately predict the internal developmental needs of their company, or when working with outside clients, help them evaluate the types of companies that they are compatible with based on their core competencies and goals. Again, it's a bit like deciding between tools. Do I need a hammer or a screw driver? Once you've assessed what will work for you, you can move forward and not give it more thought.

A company is not limited to linear cycles of growth like humans where aging eventually leads to death. A company can be revitalized through intentional "renewal". This is another area where understanding this concept can lead to strategic sophistication. You may be working for a company that has been around for 50 or 60 years, or longer. Companies that are strong and flexible renew and regenerate themselves constantly. Through renewal, companies can repeat previous stages of growth that bring new life to their business. Unlike humans, companies don't have to perish, yet so many do. They end because the ability to keep them revitalized and growing was not understood. They end because undisciplined people… people without scruples, may have caused the company's demise. Have you ever been in a company that closed its doors?

As in love, there is a company life cycle that will fit for everyone. Not every person wants to work in the chaos and low structure of a start-up company, and many people thrive within the "security" of an established, older organization. It's all a matter of taste, and just like knowing other important information about your leadership style and personal preferences, finding companies that "fit" your strengths and skill sets is critical to experiencing success as a strategic partner.

Much of the guesswork is eliminated when proposing ideas and programs to upper management (or helping others do that) because you understand the current developmental needs of your organization. It helps you and your team to make decisions because you have "criteria" that matches up with the company's needs.

Using William Bridges' work as a framework for matching up needs and strategy, the organizational phases of the Seven Phase Life Cycle looks like this:

Phase One: The Dream

This is someone's concept and it exists in a business plan. It is pure potential.

Phase Two: The Venture

The Dream takes on a physical form and a "start-up" is born. The Venture is a time of making it up as you go along, a time when hard work and commitment are critical. Job roles are fluid and evolving. The management style is seat-of-the-pants. If something looks promising, the team does it.

Phase Three: Getting Organized

Ventures can be barely a year old or 10 years old, and under the right circumstances they can become fairly large.

If they are successful, however, ventures grow to the point where they get too complicated for such looseness to work well. There are too many employees, too many customers, too much data, too much money, too many appointments, and so forth. It is going to be necessary to get organized—that is, to create systems and procedures to bring predictability to what was once just creative chaos. To not "get organized" may bring on problems related to customer service, employee relations, or financial mismanagement.

Phase Four: Making It

Barring an unusual catastrophe, a healthy venture that "Gets Organized" effectively is in a position to grow some more. But to establish itself fully as a force in its area of business requires entering a new developmental phase in which it really "Makes It." This is a dynamic stage.

Phase Four can last a long time, and in notably successful organizations, it does. It corresponds to the productive middle years of an individual's life. But just as even the most vital person continues to age and eventually slows down, organizations have a natural tendency to turn in a new direction. The vitality of Making It slowly gives way to Becoming an Institution.

Phase Five: Becoming an Institution

In this new phase, the organization may continue to be very successful. In a public sense, it may even reach new heights of success. Within its particular industry or profession, it becomes not just a successful organization, but also a familiar constellation in the organizational sky. It becomes part of the establishment, and imperceptibly, it "becomes an institution".

Everyone starts to agree that the status quo is working for them. How things are done begins to be more important than what is done. It becomes important to be "one of us" and there is a diminishing concern for productivity or effectiveness as the emphasis on alignment increases. At first this may be very subtle. The maverick star may have a great sales record, but the star person who is not "one of us" may be eased out the door.

Phase Six: Closing In

Phase six is really only a deepening of phase five. The organization not only protects the status quo, it also begins to imitate itself and turns self-imitation into a virtue. Discordant information from the outside—such as increasing numbers of complaints or the news that a competitor is launching a new product line—get filtered out or watered down so that it is of little concern. The self-centeredness of the organization becomes so strong that customers are made to feel that the organization may be doing them a favor by even serving them!

This extreme aversion to customer service takes many forms. If there is a product, a kind of perverse pride in poor quality or poor service may develop—as though service and quality were pandering to weaknesses.

If it is a government agency firmly operating within Phase Six, the citizen is made to feel that the agency is going out of its way if it even notes a request or a complaint.

Paperwork becomes an end in itself, and outdated procedures turn every undertaking into an endurance test for someone seeking assistance or information.

Phase Seven: Death

The government agency may be kept alive on the support systems of tax-fed income, but for most other organizations, phase six does not last very long. The organization dies. And organizational life continues in the same way that individual life continues: One generation disappears and another takes its place.

A dozen new ventures, based on "doing it better," may appear.

* * *

Four Avenues of Renewal

Rather than growing old and dying, an organization can renew itself and revert to an earlier stage. Renewal can happen in one of four ways:

1. A New Dream Can Be Generated
2. New Ventures Can Be Launched
3. Lost Energies Can Be Recovered
4. External Ventures or Organizations Can Be Acquired

But for our purposes we will not go into details about these now. Please refer to either of William Bridges' books: <u>The Character of Organizations</u> or to <u>Managing Transitions</u> for more about renewal.

A Time and a Place for Different Strategies

You can match a strategy to a life cycle phase. Matching your strategies to your phase will help you plan appropriate "phase specific" action steps. For this reason, there is a time and place for every new idea. The following are some examples of how a Life Cycle Phase does or doesn't match up with a good idea whose time has not come.

> **Phase Two: The Venture** A Phase Two operation doesn't need a lot of top heavy management, or a formal training department yet. However, by the time the company reaches Phase Three or Phase Four, they are more likely to be interested in that amount of structure and support. If you feel you

can't handle a lack of structure and dislike ambiguity, don't accept a position with a company in Phase Two. They aren't the ones making the mistake; it's you.

Phase Five: Becoming an Institution: Promoting the idea of standardization or economies of scale won't be "heard" when a company is in its early stages. However, those will be music to their ears in Phase Five. Make sure you align your ideas and strategies appropriately.

So that you are not wasting your time proposing and partnering strategically to deaf ears and glazed-over eyes, here are some practice questions that will help you hone your ideas to the correct life cycle phase:

1. In which phases of the life cycle would the leadership team in a company most likely welcome help with career development, leadership training, and succession planning?
2. At what point, might top sales people (or even I.T. people) become discouraged or chased out for being disruptive or too high maintenance?
3. Are there phases where companies might be less likely to invest in an internal fleet of trucks or company cars?
4. At which phases might you find that everyone is "one big family"?
5. In which phase would a company stop to audit and attempt to standardize the downloading of acceptable software on company equipment?
6. In which phases might strategic planning be welcomed and distinguished from operational planning?
7. In which phase might merging or acquiring another company seem attractive?

Answers:

1. Primarily in Phase 5, but possibly in Phases 3 or 4: it will depend on the size and progressiveness.
2. Phase 5
3. Many companies that are not transportation companies will lease their vehicles first, although some companies will provide their top people with company cars. It depends on the industry, but Phases 1, 2 and 3 are the least likely to invest in their own fleet.
4. The resounding answer is Phase 2, but "one big family" could continue into Phases 3 and 4.
5. Most likely Phases 3-4 but it could take longer than it should when the audit has to include anything after past Phase 2. After Phase 2, guidelines and uniformity are best introduced.
6. Hopefully in Phase 1, possibly in Phase 4, and again hopefully in a Renewal Phase. Many companies think they are creating a strategic plan and it's actually a form of Operational Planning tied to budgets and tactics.
7. Only in a Renewal Phase which might originate out of a Phase 4-6.

Warning: Often a mismatch occurs when a merging company in Phase 5-6, unknowingly crushes a younger company instead of experiencing the intended "renewal. The younger phased company isn't strong enough to inspire the stodgy older company back to its younger days. When no strategy or plan is in place to assure that the younger company's culture is protected, then the merger/acquisition fails and often the younger company is ruined by the experience.

Timing Is Everything

Understanding Life Cycle Phases can help you be more strategic about your career, timing of proposals, and the appropriateness of your ideas "...When you recall the jobs you have worked, which Life Cycle Phases do they represent? Were your skills well matched to the phases of the companies where you worked?"

Can you think of times in the past when because you didn't understand about "company fit" your innovative ideas or decisions may have fallen on deaf ears? If you could go back in time, would you approach selling your ideas any differently now that you know more about business life cycle phases?

*   *   *

NEXT: To further explore the resourceful side of strategizing, in the next chapter we'll examine various initiatives that are in themselves strategic because of the potential impact they have on the long-term stability of the company.

Chapter 7:
Creating Strategic Initiatives

*"Change is just a moment in time.
Transition is the mental and
emotional adjustment to the change.*

*Successful transition is the glue that secures
a lasting change. In business, we often try
to ignore and shorten the adjustment
period that would have locked in our success."*

SOMETIMES, I AM asked for examples of what is considered "strategic". I realize that it can be a bit confusing when you are new to this. But I want to reassure you that you only need to apply a very simple formula for keeping everything straight:

- Tactical action steps are about "doing" a task
- Strategic thinking is about choosing "to be" a certain way (behave, believe, become)

Which is which?

1. Meeting with an EAP vendor to discuss having an EAP program is tactical. Establishing an EAP program for the welfare of the employees and their families is strategic.
2. Meeting with the employees to update them on the state of the business is tactical. Deciding that you value communicating the state of the business to your employees (on a regular basis) is strategic.
3. Having a training department is strategic in nature because it is a commitment to the development of others. Giving the training is tactical.

Does Your Boss See Dead People?

There's a 25-year complaint floating around that goes like this: "They don't invite me to the table." "How do I get invited into the Boardroom to sit as an equal at the conference room table?" "They just don't respect me or my role." "They just don't see my value."

There's hurt on both sides. There's your hurt and then there's your boss' confusion: a big blank, innocent face of a boss who wouldn't do anything intentionally to slight a team mate. Bosses often look confused and concerned.

Another version: I see bosses get irritated and turned off because *no one likes a whiner.* "What the heck are you bellyaching about anyway?" "We can't have 20 people in those meetings." "Some people will be uncomfortable talking about their employees with you in there."

Occasionally, the whining works and you get a seat at the table. But to your amazement, nothing changes once you are inside. It's not like you thought it would be, which is very confusing. Even inside the room and sitting awkwardly at *the table* you can't seem to make any impact. Has this ever happened to you? Do you know what I am talking about? It's not what you thought it would be. Why not?

You Heard It Here First

The thinking and talking that is going around many boardroom tables is often anything but strategic. In reality, you're going to find there's more vanilla flavored discussion than you'd expect, and it can be difficult to add anything strategic to the conversation.

This, of course, is an opportunity as you build on your strategic thinking skills, to learn how to "listen between the lines" by thinking strategically and pointing out strategic aspects of their conversation that they may not have considered. For instance, is it strategic or tactical to lay off employees? It's both. Tactically, you are going to gain some cost savings. Strategically, you are going to cause some morale problems on several fronts. This is where your unique perspective can be valuable.

Assume the Role of SME

You have to START looking at yourself as a Subject Matter Expert (SME) or you won't survive. What is your "subject matter"? Is it the STRATEGIC VERSION of Operations (often the dumping ground for saving the day and fixing mistakes and delays), or is it Human Resources, the people side of the conversation, or is it managing a specific technical group? Either way, YOU need to become the SME of Strategic Thinking.

The challenge is to find ways to get YOUR strategic perspective added to the criteria for making a sound business decision, but first you have to understand what that perspective is. What are your big picture issues? What affects the success of a companywide project? You may need to have 1:1 conversations with stakeholders outside of the decision making meetings to get your point across.

In any big project, it is critical to foster employee morale, promote employee productivity and guarantee timely updates and communication; although labor intensive, building a community with the team is critical to your success. Without the cooperation and involvement of the employees and their teams, your chances of successfully moving any major change through the business will be undermined by your lack of collaboration and transparency.

Again, if you read William Bridges' work, you learn that change is just a moment in time. Transition is the mental and emotional adjustment to the change. Transition is the glue that makes a change "stick", and too often we rush or ignore taking the time for human adjustment. In the case of an Operations Department, the leader needs to speak up about available resources, or overtime implications, and about available manpower. As an observer, you can ask about these things and help each department look beyond their immediate tasks. Your point of view needs to be one of helping your teammates win against limited time and resources. When you support their success, they will realize they need you in the room.

Case Study: Winning by Default

Keep in mind that you may become a successful strategic partner by being the ONLY one who is not thinking tactically. What is really amazing is that 50% to 90% of the time, the issue of a bigger picture, or a long term consequence, is not considered when planning a new initiative. You may be the only one who is the voice of reason or at least slows them down long enough to think about consequences and forgotten details. These big picture details are not on their radar, even though they SHOULD be.

I was once in a meeting of leaders who were discussing the purchase of 150 properties of varying sizes and commercial types. They were outdoor properties. Some properties were in good shape and some weren't. They were discussing what they would fix at each property first. I was listening as a leadership advisor. I asked: "Is there a limit to the budget you have?" The top guy perked up and said, "Oh yeah, I forgot to tell you guys...you only have $250,000 to fix things!" The stunned Project Leader realized that they would have to set priorities; some properties would remain in disrepair. Ultimately, he invited me to attend all the meetings for managing the transfer of these properties to our company.

So I attended all the meetings. Many of the sale-transfer transactions were conducted over speaker phone in a conference room. The other company would ask a question. Our guys would snicker and look at each other, and possibly roll their eyes...they might rock a bit in their chairs, and possibly not say anything or speak in short sentences after a long pause. On a speaker phone it was almost impossible to read the audience.

I pulled them aside: "The people on the speaker phone can't see you. They don't know you. If you are unintentionally being disrespectful, what do you need to do differently?"

I had to make a case for crisply delivered, serious business responses to the other company's business questions. They felt the other group was being too worrisome and tactical and didn't see a reason to respond to dumb questions. I was looking at it long range and strategically. If they were going to remain competitive allies in the future, what was the extreme importance of being respectful and responsive?

Business as Un-usual

So many meetings consist of one or two people trying to get their business solutions accepted by their peer group. There's a prevailing "let's get done and get out or here" impatience in the air. The disagreements are based on approaches from diverse disciplines. There is no Desired State implied or shared vision for the meetings or the way the company is run.

The problem with this is that the group in general feels rushed; there is an unspoken concern that asking questions or exploring may irritate others who want to get back to work. To avoid this type of tone, the group leader needs to set an agenda and a goal for the discussion. Then everyone will understand the purpose of each meeting.

Early on, attempts at strategic conversation may be tactical conversations. Changing the focus of the conversation is not a switch that flips on easily. There needs to be permission to correct the focus and defer tactical suggestions; perhaps a flip chart with a Parking Lot list that can be revisited later?

Strategic thinking imagines being in the present or past tense as if it has happened. That allows your brain to look back and consider what was important to do. Reorienting your mind and conversation in this way can be frustrating at first. If the majority of the people in the room are tactical thinkers and problem solvers, it can be an uphill battle to get your point across without lots of group practice and unity. With practice, the conversations will go faster as expertise is built.

Certain verbal skillsets may be needed:

- What are two or three ways to politely redirect a tactical conversation?
- Are you willing to help others move their tactics to a bigger vision through active listening?
- Can you get your group to write down your Desired State as it develops?
- Would you know how to ask permission to broaden their conversation if they are discussing tactical solutions (doing) while struggling with "being" strategic first?

If you are the Human Resources person, or from a stakeholder department, you have an obligation to help your team mates explore the implications of their decisions whenever you see it happening. In many cases, it will be up to you and you alone, to take the conversation to a strategic place. A place it wouldn't go without you in the room. This is the role of a strategic partner.

Why Your Boss Wants You to Be Strategic

Your boss doesn't need you "going tactical" when everyone else in the room is already there. Your boss needs the counter point from you. Sometimes bosses are adept at being strategic and sometimes they are not. Either way, they need your help to create balance.

We tend to assume that everyone else in the room is more strategic than we are; which most likely isn't true 90% of the time. If you are being blamed, it's because your support is needed. If you reexamine what is going on, you will see that the blame is most likely covering up a plea for help from the top.

Not for the Faint of Heart

Once you master your skill set and build your reputation as able to think strategically, your team may see you wrinkle your brow or give a concerned smile and they'll "remember" that you are there to remind them to think strategically.

As a strategic partner, you will need to take risks. You may need to have preliminary conversations outside of the meetings to determine how far you can go with your comments and perceptions, and you will have to be thick skinned during those times when you are blatantly ignored. Being a strategic partner is an "earned" position, and it takes courage to get started and to play with the big boys and girls. Last point: It isn't important for you to win…it's only important to score. Say your piece and if they aren't ready, you'll need to score again later. Eventually, they will realize that everyone wins when they plan strategically before going tactical.

Some Companies Don't Value Strategic Thinking

You may be in a company that absolutely doesn't want ANY of the kind of help other than to be tactical. If that's the case, then you can bet they have never been sued, have not yet lost millions of dollars to a customer or employee law suit or struggled to control operating costs. You need a certain kind of stomach for this kind of company. However, the first time that one of those real life operations issues rears its ugly head, you could find your intrinsic value on the team shift if you have been patient with them.

Let's say that you have been able to establish your position as a partner. Just the existence of specific types of programs and processes serves as evidence that a company is thinking and behaving strategically. These types of landmark programs can help anchor your company's success. But they also need to match the Life Style Phase of the company.

Strategic programs and initiatives signal to others—investors, boards, shareholders and employees—by the very nature of their existence, that the company is thinking ahead and planning for the future, not just fighting fires or basking in the moment.

Examples of Strategic Initiatives—BEING versus DOING

In the following examples, the strategy is stated first (BE-coming). The bullets are the implementation steps (DO-ing):

1. Being an aligned and engaged work force

   - Write an Employee Handbook.
   - Assure the policies and procedures are clear and reflect the company goals.
   - Handbook contents are communicated to all employees.
   - Supervisors are given appropriate training on how to carry out the policies.

- Employees are asked to sign off on "receipt" of their copy of the Handbook.

2. A strong leadership team in a learning organization

   - Hiring is reflective of Success Factors or Company Values.
   - The team has a strategic plan that aligns their decisions and behaviors.
   - A Succession Plan & Talent Review program drives development and talent management.
   - Development Plans promote learning and growth and promote job retention.
   - National tracking of talent creates career opportunities for cross-training or promotion.
   - Develop formally documented "success factors" that spell out minimum levels of engagement and interpersonal expertise (hierarchical levels may be: individual contributor, supervisor, middle manager, and senior manager). May also include additional technical or functional-specific success factors that spell out competency levels. These success factors are at the heart of all career advancement decisions and promote uniformity and scalability

3. Market leader with high customer and employee retention rates

   - Set YOY (year over year) market growth rates.
   - Introduce innovative marketing programs to attract desired demographics.
   - Conduct the research and data needed to focus on top three demographic growth areas.
   - Reduce customer churn by X percent, YOY.
   - Reduce employee turnover. Improve retention by introducing an Employee Development program.
   - Introduce training for employees on new technology that will be needed.

- 18 months in, if all goals are met: hold company-wide celebration at exciting venue.
- Gain sharing program introduced after 2-3 years of success.

4. Define and implement Operational Excellence:

- Attain it in 36 months in gradual steps.
- Introduce the use of Project Managers for key projects.
- Expand current use of Systems Thinking techniques, train more employees.
- Increase Quality Assurance initiatives in key areas.
- Initiate Portfolio Management.
- Assure Organizational Development support.

These are examples of strategic initiatives that you can consider when the time is right. What types of initiatives is your company currently driving? You may see that strategic opportunities seem to be coming from the Human Resources Department. If they are not, they need to be. That implies that your HR leader needs to have a strategic mind. Why do you think this is important? I think it's important because many of the problems in functional departments are tactical: SME (subject matter expert) types of problems. In Human Resources, there is an orientation towards "being" a certain way on the behalf of the employees. The same is true in Marketing for the customers and as it relates to branding, and may be true in Government Regulatory departments where being seen as aligned with government directives is valued.

When the Operations, Finance, and Sales departments become more strategic, they also become more collaborative. They have to; that's what a shared Desired State does; it promotes team focus and communications.

Remember to consider the Life Cycle phase of your company. Don't chase ideas and work that doesn't fit the needs of your current company's goals and development needs.

It will be important to socialize your ideas and craft your proposals in appropriate strategic language for your stakeholders or boss. From a political standpoint, it's never just your boss that needs the strategic perspective; you have peers and subordinates who also need your influence and inspiration.

Metrics and tracking are also a part of partnering strategically, so grab some of the good books out there that tell you which metrics to track and how to use them in a meaningful way. Remember, however, that just tracking metrics is still tactical (doing). And that it's important (and strategic) to have metrics that are consistent across all stakeholder groups so that each team can understand the progress being made.

What will be created by your efforts? As you work to improve your department's functionality and your company's future with those metrics, what else will become possible? How will you communicate your goals to your staff? Being able to answer these types of questions will be what defines your success as a strategic partner.

*   *   *

NEXT: We are going to tie everything we've discussed into a story illustrating the challenges of taking risks to partner with others when behaving strategically isn't a well-developed skill. This is Mike's story.

Chapter 8:
A Perfect Example

"If a person is not 'ready'
to hear a message or to collaborate,
you can't do much about it.
Remain approachable and
non-defensive."

The Company:

THIS IS A story about GummedUp, Inc. and five of their key employees. GummedUp is a well-funded, start-up mining and exploration company. They've been together less than a year. There are about 30 people in the organization, most of whom are highly educated professionals.

GummedUp is like many small businesses, or large departments, it thrives on the brains and dedication of its caring individuals. But these professionals are not aligned or supported by their GM.

The Key Players:

1. *The General Manager:*

   - Lacks the experience and leadership awareness to focus his team on results and collaboration.
   - Works with team mates as individuals and not as his cross functional mastermind group.
   - Spends time holed up in his office rather than engaging and communicating with his employees.
   - Lately, appears frustrated and angry with team. Is his job being criticized behind the scenes?

2. *Grace, Human Resources*

   Grace is about ready to throw in the towel. As the person who coordinates the hiring and firing, she feels undermined and unappreciated by just about everyone in her company, especially her GM. It is his attitude that prompts other department heads to treat Grace's department like it is a dumping ground for last minute decisions, dysfunctional behavior and bending the rules.

   Grace has tried to talk to the GM about all the hiring that is going on. The company is running out of floor space. She needs to be included in the interviews, and she needs to be alerted when someone new has been hired and will be starting work so she can be prepared. However, she's not been able to get anyone to respect her wishes or help her out.

Grace is concerned about employee morale and potential liabilities. She's reached out to the GM about her concerns, but he acted annoyed as if she doesn't know how to do her job. She doesn't like being yelled at or ignored, and both are happening. Recently, she has scaled down her expectations and is playing it safe. She doesn't want to create any more trouble for anyone, especially herself.

3. *Susan, Executive Assistant to the General Manager*

Seems to have "inside" information; knows more about what's really going on than anyone.

4. *Brent, the "unofficial" VP*

- He is one of the few who doesn't seem to be in trouble; his status is confusing. He is feared.
- Flies below the radar, turns up MIA (Missing in Action) when chaos hits.
- Doesn't disclose much, but is a good listener and seems sincere.
- The team suspects that he has been demoralized at some point.
- He oversees large company projects; he's been involved with several failed projects that the GM has lead.

5. *Mike, I.T. Leader with VP status*

- Highest ranking person under the GM, although he doesn't appear to have GM support.
- Was aggressively recruited by Brent and the GM. For this reason, he wonders if the GM is fired, will his job be secure?
- Has a reputation for being annoying because he tries to work around the GM.

- Constantly comes to HR with questions and concerns that HR doesn't seem ready or able to address.
- Doesn't seem empowered by the organization; lacks the tools to succeed.
- GM puts him down in meetings in front of his colleagues.
- He seems like an acceptable leader who wants to get things organized, but HR and the other leaders are tired of being in trouble with their grouchy GM, so they resist Mike's efforts to move forward. They want to know: "Did the GM approve this?"
- Mike hits lots of brick walls with this group.

The Situation:

Mike, the VP of I.T., knows that Susan has been helping the GM make appointments to preview other office buildings that might be big enough to house their growing employee base. There is a rumor about moving, and the timing keeps switching from "next week" to "not at all". Additionally, there is no information about "what part of town", or whether responsibility for logistics will fall on Mike's team. With Mike being excluded from the planning, it is possible to assume that Mike might not be responsible for moving their company. Mike has not been directly told anything. This doesn't sit well with Mike.

Mike knows that moving people isn't going to be an overnight task and that work stations will have to be quickly moved and reassembled in some logical order by a team of people. Mike has come from a more mature company where he was accustomed to collaboration and team work. He's talked to Grace about his logistical concerns several times, but he's been unable to get Grace to partner with him.

Mike also suspects that the GM is on his way "out", and that it is just a matter of time (and timing) before he is let go. The clues are:

- The company just lost 20% of the millions of dollars they had been funded in several bad deals that the GM spearheaded.

- The GM is spending a lot of time alone in his office and he is even more agitated than usual.
- The GM yelled at two corporate visitors; and is refusing to work with them.
- The GM lost his right to oversee the work of his project manager because there was a corporate person who is now on the premises evaluating the failure of the last projects and the selection of future projects; and
- The GM is not authorized to oversee or negotiate any further deals.

Given this may be an impending event, it is hard to imagine that they will be moving, but at the same time, more people are still being hired and floor space for new work stations is almost gone. Of course, there is always the option that once the GM leaves, others will be fired also...thus, freeing up some floor space...so assuming he could be asked at the last minute to orchestrate a location move, Mike began to develop several "moving and staying" options.

Mike felt that if he didn't do something different and do it quickly, he would be swept out with his GM (and possibly Brent) when the changing of the guard occurred. Although it was speculation, so was the moving rumor, so Mike worked to collaborate with Grace, Susan, and Brent on developing a scenario plan for several possible options. He knew he had to stop working in a silo. The working conditions really couldn't be much worse so there was not a lot to lose by taking a fresh approach.

How Mike Partnered

Mike's approach was three-pronged. He worked harder to build rapport with Susan, Grace and Brent. Each relationship was planned based on their needs, personalities, and what he perceived was their experience. He reduced his own political isolation by reaching out. He prepared himself emotionally for some upfront rejection. If they didn't respond favorably right away, he would be patient and stay focused...hoping that they'd come around after they had an opportunity to think about the advantages of collaborating.

- He began by talking to each of them about their functional responsibilities and looked for ways to be of assistance.
- He offered to help them from their point of view while sharing his concerns, and showing them how his department could help address their concerns.
- Mike's focus was to help them be successful in their current roles.
- He started by checking in with Susan to be sure that she still believed that the move could happen. Mike explained his concerns from the standpoint of cost per work station, planning for additional room, employee morale, and the importance of having some logistics planning meetings with him, their I.T. leader.
- He supported Susan by offering her background on what his department would have to do to make the move go smoothly. He provided her with enough information to advise the General Manager so their GM might also make good decisions. Mike hoped that by doing this, Susan would remind the GM that Mike needed lead time and authority to get them moved safely and without business interruption.

Next, Mike met with Brent to try to get some background on the direction of the company.

- Mike shared his concerns about the employee morale and logistics issues with Brent who listened intently but didn't say much.
- Mike wanted to use the move as an opportunity to clean up the software abuse issues. He asked Brent his opinion on how far he could push the GM for support and increased communication. If Brent was helpful, then he would move forward to Grace with these additional insights. If Brent

couldn't help, then Mike would still speak with Grace, but possibly with a less robust proposal.

With Grace, he wanted to discuss the possibility of a move and the implications it could have on her department. If the move was announced suddenly, it could cause employee relations problems (morale, resentment, inconveniences and interrupted projects).

- What kind of help would she like from him now?
- What were her concerns?
- How could they collaborate on a delivery plan in case a move was announced? He would explain how long he thought it would take him to implement the move from beginning to end, discuss the potential cost, and gather her ideas on staging the event. Who should go first? Where did she anticipate resistance? What else could she think of?

Not only was Mike reaching out to partner with three colleagues who were as isolated as he was, but he was also building his reputation as a "proactive" strategic thinker, and a concerned leader. Mike was also clearing up the potential for someone to say, "I don't really know what Mike does all day". If the GM was eliminated, one of these people (or all of them) would be able to stand up for Mike's value and role in the organization. Until he tried to reach out to the three of them, it would have been difficult for them to politically support him, and vice versa.

Mike's Results

Susan welcomed the logistics strategies and the bigger picture that Mike offered. She liked Mike's support for her role. To be honest she was a little intimidated by all that was happening. She was impressed with Mike's organizational approach, his big picture skills and his down-to-earth way of explaining technical aspects of the move. Later if the GM tried to pull the trigger on a move, she would be able to slow him down by convincing him to consult with Mike on implementation and timing.

Brent at first only listened and wasn't able to help. Mike was tempted to be afraid of Brent politically. But within a few days, Brent voluntarily approached Mike with some feedback on how to more effectively reach the GM (which days, on which subjects, and some inside information on how to talk to him). This helped Mike refine his approach.

Grace, it turned out, had not heard the moving rumors and went into panic mode. Mike was reassuring and offered to brainstorm with her. At first, she was irritated with Mike for considering such an idea as moving. Once she discovered that Susan also had the same concerns, she realized that Mike was trying to help her and be preemptive. She circled back around and apologized for her reactions and they began to brainstorm several potential scenarios. They planned several different scenarios, including the possibility that if the move occurred, they might not be able to control the timing.

Even if the GM gave no warning, they would be prepared. Grace would intensify her one-on-one contact with department heads and independent groups as needed. While Mike and his team moved equipment and got it back up and running as soon as possible, she would keep the communication flowing to the employees until everything was under control. Susan and she would partner, too. Finally, Grace would have two people with whom she could talk to. She liked the new arrangement because now she was learning other parts of the business, and she finally had some political support. Mike's and Grace's efforts worked to make Susan's role successful in the eyes of the employees, too. Susan appreciated that.

What Mike Learned

Mike learned about patience and about human behavior:

- If a person is not 'ready' to hear a message or to collaborate, you can't do much about it. What works best in a situation like the one he faced with Brent is to confidently present your request and information, and then calmly stand back, remaining approachable and non-defensive.

- Most people will forget how difficult they were, and remember that you remained approachable. This gives them the opportunity to circle back around with you. Allowing people to save face is very important. Compassion for other's fear or hesitation is also very important.

- Most things said in conflict are a form of stress reaction. Many people have no concept of how stressed out they become – they just chock it up to being mad at you. They aren't aware that stress causes them to become difficult, rude, or inappropriate. Since they have control over their filters and reactions to the conflict interaction, they carry most of the sole responsibility for their reactions in stressful situations. Mike was ready to remain above all of this.

- What Mike needed help with was how to get started. Once he found his way, his situation started to improve rapidly. His strategic approach was born out of his frustration and an almost desperate need to relieve a very frustrating work situation.

* * *

NEXT: Where do we start to become more strategic? Your starting point is probably the last place you would think to look.

Chapter 9:
The Starting Point

"The Way Forward...

'Some said that it couldn't be done.
He with a chuckle replied,
Maybe it couldn't, but he'd be the one
Who wouldn't say so till he tried.
So he lifted his chin with a slip of a grin
On his face, if he worried, he hid it.
And he started to sing as he tackled the thing
That couldn't be done and he did it.'"

—Edgar Guest "the people's poet"

T's POSSIBLE THAT by now you are thinking either that you won't ever be able to learn this, or that you are eager to start practicing to be a better strategic partner. Some of you, in fact, may have started to search the Internet for books or classes that will help you develop your skills beyond this book.

Making Strategy More Right Brain

I DO have another book to recommend that is delightful reading and could be very helpful to those of you who are serious. You won't be surprised that I like this author's work. It's by a well-known British strategist named Bob Gorzynski (http://TheSpiritofStrategy.org). He is the Director at the Centre for Strategic Thinking, an author, a consultant, and strategic coach. His approach is holistic and creative. Gorzynski's book The Strategic Mind helps us "experience"what a strategic mind looks, sounds and feels like. If you like analogies that reference stories from Winnie the Pooh, episodes from the television show "Friends," and poetic ditties that will make you smile, you will enjoy Bob Gorzynski's book very much. He takes a lot of the mystery out of this valuable skill set and will help you integrate strategy into your imagination and heart.

The poem preceding this chapter is borrowed from his book. I dedicate it to each of you as you embark on your journey. Give yourself time to integrate what we have discussed and set your intention on developing your mental skills.

Give yourself a year. Write down in a journal how you feel today and the feedback that you are getting currently. In a year, visit that page and update your status. Have you grown professionally? Are your opinions valued? Do you hear conversations differently? Are you getting complimentary feedback?

However, hear me on this: classes and books are not the only or first place to start! You need to start wherever you are…if you are in a very tactical mind set, start from that point.

Flexing Your Muscles

Going back to what we discussed in Chapter 5 (Convincing Tactical Thinkers to Go Strategic), begin to experiment with the "DO versus BE" dichotomy. Although it's a bit counter intuitive to start with the tactical, it can actually be the "sweet spot" for developing future success. When your boss or your team is talking about what they want to DO, flex your mind muscle and ask yourself calmly:

- "If they DO this, where will they BE in one year?"
- "If we keep DO-ing this, what will we BE-come?"
- "If our company continues down this path, what will our customers (or our employees) begin to BE-lieve about us?"

Every time, you find yourself in a tactical conversation, choose to hear the conversation differently by asking yourself any or all of these three questions. Practice in silence. Or write down the decisions and after the meeting, complete this exercise. In no time flat, you will be seeing the difference between DO and BE and you will be able to begin to express your insights through questions to your team or boss.

Your questions will probably need to be prefaced with obtaining "permission to explore a different point of view" which most people will eagerly grant you out of pure curiosity! But you have to think to ask! Asking softens the exercise of potentially seeing the solution differently.

Building Trust

A strategic thinker is someone who makes good use of tactical conversations. They don't shun tactical thinking or run away from something that is unproductive, they help translate and transform the group mind. The goal is to build everyone's trust and confidence as you promote strategic thinking and help the group (or individual) challenge their own beliefs and assumptions.

As your skills progress, you can expect to be asked to these tactical meetings as a valuable resource. To give you an example, I have been told by bosses, "PLEASE speak up at these meetings! I am waiting to hear from you. It MATTERS what you think, and I always appreciate your perspective."

Even your silence can be powerful. Either it is a display of approval, or the look on your face (combined with the silence) can have a powerfully sobering effect on a group that is running amuck. Eventually, they will look over at you (because you are not in the same energetic mode that they are) and realize, "Oh ?%!, we better ask her how SHE sees it (before we schedule the victory party!)."

Case Study:

Once, in a very large conference room with many teammates around me, I heard five department heads, leaders of my company, starting to go down a tactical path that could have many negative repercussions for other functional groups or even our customers. Since we have a preexisting agreement that it's my job to speak up if I see them becoming too tactical, I bolstered my courage and I spoke up. All I said was, "I don't hear a clear Desired State; all I hear is problem solving. What's the end game?"

I couldn't see them, and they couldn't see me, but they heard my "voice of reason" coming from the back of the crowded conference room. If they didn't know I was in the room, now they did. All the nonsense stopped dead when another person (who I'd never met but who turned out to be a leader in the finance department) said, "Yeah, what's the Desired State?"

The conversation shifted and we were out of potential trouble. About a month later, two of the female middle managers pulled me aside in a room with no witnesses. It was a thrilling-scary moment—almost like being interrogated: dark room, spot lights, two-on-one. These two were on a mission. "Girl, we WANT what you HAVE! What did you DO to those leaders that day?! Those five sat up straight in their chairs and shook their heads like you'd thrown water on them! Nothing was the same after that. What's that about?!"

What it was "about" was I had:

1. pre-existing permission to speak up,
2. an agreement that we are going to try to be "strategic think-ers" not tactical thinkers,
3. pre-existing trust and established credibility, and
4. the courage to (even in front of many strangers) remind my leaders of OUR agreements and that we valued hav-ing a strategy before making decisions, no matter how sexy the idea.

The behavior of these two curious middle managers' was an eye opener for me. I hadn't seen what they saw. I hadn't realized the full impact of my actions until they confronted me.

Silence Works Too

When you don't have anything to add, then it can imply (at least) two things:

1. Either the group must be on the right track, or
2. You aren't buying the process and thus are holding back.

Often, they will look over at you, and stop dead…"what???" (as in "What did I do now?")

Be reassuring, be humble and ask permission to ask some ques-tions. When you have buy-in and curiosity, gently question their beliefs and assumptions about the bigger picture and whether the solution matches the vision.

The most common response after I finish sharing my concerns is:

- "Oh, I never thought about that…good point."
- "Damn! You ask such killer questions. Hell, I don't know how to answer that!
- "That's a GOOD question! I wish I'd thought of THAT!" or my favorite,
- "Yikes, you bring up a good point! That probably is what is wrong. How do I get out of this?"

The Bottom Line

Whether you are participating in a group or are talking one-on-one, this is all about helping others make better decisions by partnering with them. Hopefully they will learn to collaborate with you proactively but as you can see that doesn't always happen. Over time, these are your goals:

- Becoming a trusted colleague who can be depended on to offer up clear, authentic feedback.
- Creating a space for your audience to think out their ideas while you are acting with empathy and level-headed wisdom.
- Aiding others to stretch their thinking and shift their perspective without shame
- Helping others learn to address and implement win-win solutions whenever they involve highly sensitive employee/people issues.
- When there are ethical considerations, being the one who holds the high standards and sparks "right action" even if it's going to be publicly embarrassing or difficult in some way.
- Spurring good ideas and innovation – helping others explore their beliefs and assumptions without a vested interest in the outcome.
- Allowing for some discussion of personal impact or issues that may be affecting work performance and outcomes.

- Creating a safe place for wrestling with important decisions or Big Hairy Goals.
- Help your teammates consider the pros and cons, explore innovative thinking and imagine their Desired State.

What It Takes

Collaboration is a skillset in today's market place. The courage to visualize business outcomes and to articulate them is essential for priceless work experiences. Strategy is a collective dream. Becoming strategic is a collaborative journey.

About the Author

TIMI GLEASON IS a global Leadership Coach and Strategic Thinking mentor. She holds Gold Mastery Certification in Strategic Management and Systems Thinking from the Haines Centre, a global strategic planning firm. Timi spent more than 15 years in Fortune 500 and Family Owned HR Leadership positions with experience in Organizational Development, Training and Development, Leadership Coaching and HR Mentoring. She also has 15 years of experience serving on traditional strategic planning teams.

Over the years, Timi has developed her own unique, exciting strategic planning programs designed to specifically engage and empower teams and boards so that strategic plans do not sit and gather dust on a shelf. She has used these processes with both for-profit businesses and non-profit agencies. Her goal is to increase strategic planning globally and to make it accessible to new users.

Additionally, Timi speaks and writes about leadership and professional development topics. She is a Master Career Coach with certifications in Stakeholder Centered Coaching (the Marshall Goldsmith method), Community Mediation, Creative Leadership (Creative Problem Solving Institute/CPSI from Buffalo State University), and is a past two-time Rotary Club president.

Timi lives in Southern California and is the proud mom of Gen X and Gen Y leaders, Kevin and Kristin, who do not fall far from their mother's apple tree.

strategycoach@executivegoals.com

Need Timi's Help?

1. Mentoring: Strategic Thinking and the Art of Developing a Desired State
2. Training on the basic Systems Thinking formula used in Strategic Planning and Thinking
3. Finding Your Voice: becoming more articulate in front of peer groups
4. Business Acumen Development: understanding cross-functional priorities and differences in business focus
5. Virtual Strategic Planning™ – a 21st century approach to planning for remote locations and busy team members
6. Crowd-Sourced Strategic Planning™–partnering with geographically dispersed organizations to develop a robust strategic plan, three core strategies, and hundreds of fresh approaches.
7. Strengths-Based Leadership and Strengthsfinder 2.0 team building

8. Leadership Assessments—
    - The Birkman: to study stress responses, team building, and increase self-awareness
    - Myers Briggs Type Indicator (MBTI)
    - DISC Teamwork Model
    - Your Persuasion Style
    - The Five Language of Appreciation

Email Timi at **StrategyCoach@ExecutiveGoals.com**

- Leave your contact information and time zone
- Please explain briefly which service you would like to discuss
- Suggest some best times to talk via phone or Skype.

Resources

Books (in order of their mention):

The Dip, by Seth Godin
Peaks and Valleys, by Spencer Johnson, MD
The Slight Edge, by Jeff Olson.
The Impending Crisis, by the late Roger Herman
The Five Dysfunctions of a Team, by Patrick Lencioni
Silos, Politics and Turf Wars, by Patrick Lencioni
Leadership and Self Deception: Getting Outside the Box, by the Arbinger Institute
Crucial Conversations, by Kerry Patterson, Joseph Grenny, Ron McMillan, Al Switzler, and Stephen R. Covey
The Man Who Listens to Horses, by Monty Roberts
The Character of Organizations, by William Bridges
Managing Transitions, by William Bridges
Seeing Systems: Unlocking the Mysteries of Organizational Life by Barry Oshry
The Way Forward, by Edgar Guest
The Strategic Mind, by Bob Gorzynski
Career Coaching: An Insiders' Guide, by *Marcia Bench*

Virtual Strategic Planning™

Wɪᴛʜᴏᴜᴛ ᴀ sᴛʀᴀᴛᴇɢɪᴄ plan, many organizations are like airplanes taking off without a flight plan. It is very hard to make solid decisions and to focus resources without a destination supporting your action steps. Yet, a majority of organizations attempt success without a clear plan. They may be clear about what they have to DO, but will likely never enter the process of visualizing an unforgettable destination.

To create a strategic plan requires a time commitment. That effort is similar to the one put forth in preparing for a large dinner party. It requires conceptualization, an environmental scan, a SWOT analysis of existing tools and resources, action steps and a measure of emotional investment; we want our guests to be thrilled!

Without a strategic plan, organizations fall short of their potential. They waste valuable time arm wrestling over ideas and competing for resources. How do we let this happen?

1) Strategic Plans require that we talk to each other and align our efforts. Teams that don't have a shared vision complain of being too busy and time-constrained to meet.
2) Hiring outside facilitation is often needed.
3) Strategic Plans have a reputation for sitting on the shelf and not being discussed until the next strategic planning session. When meetings are ineffective, the process of strategic planning can feel disconnected and meaningless.

Addressing these Issues with Virtual Strategic Planning™ (VSP) and Crowd Sourcing™ (CSSP)

Virtual Strategic Planning™ resolves many of these age old problems. The VSP process can be executed anywhere and happens without time constraints. Thought provoking planning questions are distributed via email. Meeting rooms, meals, hotels, and travel accommodations are unneeded.

Up to 25 people can participate effectively. Equal voice is available to all participants. Stakeholders can include current Board Members, or can be Crowd Sourced™ by including any of the following: a) previous and future board members, b) high performing volunteers, c) select donors, d) select vendors, and f) highly passionate customers or non-profit clients.

Additional types of Crowd Sourced Strategic Planning™ may include subsidiaries across national regions, and non-competing, dissimilar organizations with similar visions (Desired States). This last category promotes the diversity of ideas and perspectives. There is also a Pay-to-Play contingency that opens up opportunities to vetted altruists and philanthropists who have the ability to underwrite the partial cost of a VSP in trade for participating in the plan.

VSP Solves the Following Classic Planning Challenges

By including a broader group of respondents, an infusions of ideas and diverse perspectives brings life to your plans. During the process, participants have equal access and plenty of "thinking time" to consider the depth of each question.

Group debriefs occur in-person, or via an on-line video conferencing platform that can include up to 25 participant faces. Developing buy-in becomes a focused discussion of the recommendations and survey responses. The voice of the respondents is reflected in the finished product and consequently, consensus usually occurs quickly and easily.

The primary document is approximately five pages and can be easily referenced.

The simplicity of a Virtual Strategic Plan™ ignites engagement and promotes instant alignment. The finished product reflects everyone's heartfelt ideas and opinions in their own words.

*   *   *

*To find out more contact Timi: strategycoach@*executivegoals.com.